HOW TO WRITE AND SELL C

In this Series

Other titles in preparation

WRITE AND SELL
COMPUTER SOFTWARE

A practical guide to creating and marketing software ideas

Stephen Harding

How To Books

This book is dedicated to my wife Ruth, and to Sarah and Victoria, my two lovely daughters.

Cartoons by Mike Flanagan

British Library Cataloguing in Publication Data
A catalogue record for this book is available from the British Library.

© Copyright 1996 by Stephen Harding.

First published in 1996 by How To Books Ltd, Plymbridge House, Estover Road, Plymouth PL6 7PZ, United Kingdom.

Produced for How To Books by Deer Park Productions.
Typeset by PDQ Typesetting, Stoke-on-Trent, Staffs.
Printed and bound by The Cromwell Press Ltd, Broughton Gifford, Melksham, Wiltshire.

Contents

List of Illustrations

Preface

You want to write and sell your own computer software. Where do you start? You need to know:

- What software to write.

- How to write it.

- How and where to sell it.

Computers are everywhere nowadays – in schools, colleges, shops, banks, in the home and in the workplace. Wherever computers exist there is strong, continual demand for good quality software that enables people to make full use of their power.

This demand is met by a growing number of companies and individuals whose sole purpose is to provide the market with the quality software it needs. Surprisingly, most of this software is conceived, written and sold by very small companies and individuals who have taken an idea, developed it, written some software and offered it to the market. If they can do it then so can you.

Developing a software package for sale is great fun and, taken step-by-step, can be a simple, successful and rewarding experience.

Before reaching for your keyboards, take a little time to read this book, a practical guide which will show you how to transform your ideas into a marketable software package. It will show you how to present ideas to the market, listen to feedback, plan and write the software, document and protect your software, and most important of all, how to find your customers, how to sell your product and begin to operate a small, revenue-earning software business.

Each chapter addresses the different facet of the business of creating and selling a software package, but they all have something in common: they show how to make money from the software you write, to provide either a full-time living or just a valuable extra income earned in your spare time.

Ensuring success in any walk of life is never guaranteed, but you are much more likely to achieve success if you plan for it. It is hoped that by reading this book you can put in place the plan which will eventually lead you to successfully develop and sell your own software package.

Stephen Harding

IS THIS YOU?

Sixthform student   Fifthform student

Computer programmer

DP consultant   Project technician

PC owner

Business consultant   Freelance writer

Computer games-player

Accountant   Business manager

Marketing executive

Entrepreneur   Working from home

Systems analyst

Redundant   Unemployed

Teacher

Lecturer   College student

University student

Self-employed   Business start-up

Designer

Innovator   Enthusiast

Publisher

Editor   Computer retailer

Software buyer

Mature student   Graduate

Knowledge specialist

Management trainee   Business student

1
Getting Started

You want to write and sell your own **software**. Great. It is a wonderful way of earning money – sometimes lots of it. It is also creative, exciting, interesting and immensely satisfying to see the software that you have written being used, appreciated and paid for by others. It is hard work too, but enjoyable hard work and more than compensated by the rewards – personal and financial – that await a successful software package.

If your dream is to write and sell your own **software package**, then this book is for you. Step-by-step it will show what software to write, how to write it, how to market it and how to sell it. All you need to begin with is a vision, lots of enthusiasm and a willingness to work hard.

WRITING A SOFTWARE PACKAGE

Writing a software package simply means writing a collection of one or more **computer programs** which together perform a task, or a range of related tasks, on a computer. Software packages become popular if they are of use to people.

Popular types of software packages and their uses
Different types of software package enable computer users to perform various tasks

- **Word processors** produce letters and documents.

- **Databases** store and retrieve information.

- **Spreadsheets** easily manipulate numbers.

- **Computer games** entertain.

It is easy to see why people *want* software packages. They make life easier and more enjoyable. But what motivates people to *write* and *sell* software?

People write software because it is:

- enjoyable
- creative
- interesting
- useful
- profitable.

Writing software is actually only profitable to a very small percentage of software authors. This is because writing and selling software are two completely separate disciplines and most software authors find it much easier to write software packages than they do to sell them.

The aim here is to both write *and* sell software, so how do you begin?

Starting out

Most people start writing software by copying a few lines of **program code** onto a computer, from a book or computer magazine. Given enough time to learn and practise, most could become capable of writing a complete and usable software package. Some, maybe including yourself, already have the technical ability to start the task today, whilst others are still learning. In any case, no formal qualifications are required to write software. A logical mind, enthusiasm and hard work are far more important than academic achievements.

Selling your software

Though good programming skills, however acquired, are essential in order to create quality, saleable software, they will not in themselves guarantee you an income from the software you write. To make money from your software you have to *sell* it. This means finding customers and selling to them.

Leaving aside technical ability for the moment, what selling software involves, is selling a **product**. In order to know what kind of product your software package should be, you need to know what kind of software products customers demand and buy.

Software-buying customers

Customers only buy the software which they most want or need. They want:

- a quality product

- a reasonable price

- professional service

- peace of mind.

Quality software

Customers want to buy quality software. They want well-designed, attractively presented software which is easy to use and which does what it says it can do on the box.

A reasonable price

Price is important but not as important as quality. Customers are willing to pay a little more for quality software – indeed, they expect to.

Professional service

Customers demand professional and reliable service, and return time after time to buy from companies and individuals who deliver it.

Peace of mind

Peace of mind results when customers buy a quality product, at a reasonable price, from a professional and reliable supplier.

Thinking of the customer at all times

This is the golden rule. In order to be able to offer your customers what they want you should prepare, research, write and sell your software package *with the customer in mind at all times.*

Did you know?

1. British customers currently spend about 7 billion pounds per year on software and software-related services.

2. Only a half of all British businesses own a computer.

3. There is always room in the market for another software package.

GETTING THE THINGS YOU NEED

The process of developing software for sale can be a long one, but it can be started cheaply and easily. To start work on your new software package you will initially need:

● an idea

● pens, paper and perhaps one or two computer magazines.

What about a computer, some software, and a printer? Yes, you will need these, but not until later.

To start writing a software package you must have some idea of *who* or *what* to write it for. Your immediate task is to identify and then develop an idea for your own software package. The pens and paper are for making notes as you go.

One or two computer magazines may also be useful at this stage. Just by browsing through them, reading the latest news, features and advertisements, you can often find the seeds of an idea for a software package of your own.

FINDING THAT ALL-IMPORTANT IDEA

All computer software packages, even the most popular and well known, have started life as an idea. Finding a good idea for your own software package is probably the most important part of your whole project. The better your idea, the more chance you have of developing a saleable and successful product.

Your idea will also dictate all future stages in the development of your software package. It will determine:

● who your customers are

● what software you write

● how you advertise and sell your software

● and whether your efforts will be enjoyable and profitable.

Good software packages are not difficult to find. First, consider what kinds of software packages customers buy. You have probably bought software at some time or other yourself, so start by looking at this. It is likely that you have bought software which:

- helps you with your work
- is related to a hobby or interest you have
- is enjoyable to use.

Using software at work
People buy all sorts of software packages to help them at work, for example:

- word processors
- accounts software
- databases
- drawing software
- spreadsheets
- graphics software
- programming languages
- communications software
- project planners
- sales processing software
- mailing list software
- other custom-written software.

Answer the following questions to help you find an idea for a software package which may be of use to you in your place of work.

1. What software do you use at work?

2. What tasks do you perform manually at work which could be achieved more efficiently using a software package?

3. What software do your colleagues use and are they happy with it?

4. What software do your friends use at their places of work?

Because you already know your own job inside out, you may well be able to identify shortcomings and deficiencies in working practices and areas of your work in which the use of a software package would be beneficial.

Hobbies, sport and pastimes
Spare time pursuits and pastimes provide fertile ground for software

authors looking for that important initial idea.

If you enjoy football, then what about a software package which analyses the results of league and non-league teams or displays statistics on teams, players and managers, both past and present? If you collect stamps, then why not a software package which displays the pictures of world stamps together with their value and other details? Cricketers are obsessed with bowling and batting statistics, athletes with pace, timings and training schedules, and horse racing fans with handicaps, results and betting.

Are there any software packages you would buy now, or would buy if they were available, which you could use in pursuit of your favourite hobbies and interests? If so then maybe you have some ideas already.

Some pastimes which could be enhanced by a software package

athletics	horse racing and riding
car maintenance	indoor games
collecting antiques	investing
computer programming	keeping pets
cooking	knitting
cricket	learning a foreign language
cycling	photography
drawing	rugby
electronics	sailing
embroidery	stamp and coin collecting
fishing	studying at home
football	tennis
golfing	wood working
health and fitness	writing

Entertaining your customers

Whether they care to admit it or not, most people who have used a computer have also played computer games. Some people are games addicts.

Computer games come in many varieties, including 'shoot em-up'-type games, strategy and adventure games. Games are among the highest selling software packages and it makes good sense to at least consider the games market when looking for software ideas. Beware though; the games market is extremely competitive, and programming the games requires the highest degree of professional competence and. technical skills.

Existing software that sells

If you are still short of ideas, take a look at the current best-selling software packages. This will give you plenty of ideas for your own software. Make a list of the current best-selling software packages.

Ten ways of finding out what software is currently selling well

Computer magazines

1. Look for the software 'top twenty' charts in popular computer magazines.

2. The multi-paged adverts of the top software retailers display the most popular (highest selling) software packages.

3. Examine the reviews and features for new and existing software. The larger the review, the more popular the software is or is expected to be.

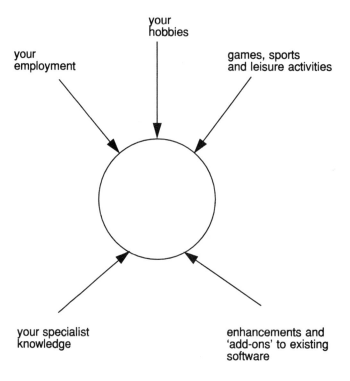

Fig. 1. Common sources of software ideas.

Talking to software users

4. Find out what software your friends and business associates use.

5. Find out what software is being used in your local schools, colleges, and small businesses.

6. Find out what software is used by local clubs or special interest groups.

7. What software is popular with the members of your local computer club?

Software retailers and book shops

8. Look at the software on sale in your local computer stores. Politely ask the proprietor which of his software lines are most popular.

9. Look at the titles on sale in one of the many new computer superstores. These are sure to be the current most popular titles.

10. Analyse the titles in the computer software section of your local book shop; it is likely that the most popular software packages are the subjects of many of the books in that section.

Popular is not always best

Most of the software packages you have just listed are probably owned and developed by some of the world's largest software companies. Because of the huge sums of money these companies have available for development and marketing, it is extremely difficult for new software authors to compete with them on equal terms. In view of this, you are well advised to make a mental note of the software packages on your list and then to steer clear of trying to directly compete with them. Your list has shown you what software to *avoid* writing; now use it to find the kinds of software *to* write.

Filling gaps in the market

Analyse the list. Are there any obvious gaps, any glaring omissions? Are there any software packages you would expect to see on the list but which are not there? If so, then, maybe you could fill the gap.

Complement and enhance

Using your list, look for ideas which, rather than mimicking the functionality of the top software packages, complement, enhance or work alongside them in some way. For example, rather than writing your own equivalent of the world's top-selling word processor, consider writing a software package which works in conjunction with the word processor, for example using the computer's sound system to 'read' aloud the document that you have just written.

Producing enhancements, or **add-ons** as they are sometimes known, to existing, top-selling products, can be very lucrative because many of the purchasers of the original product are likely to be interested.

Specialising: finding a niche

Many smaller software companies produce software which, rather than trying to satisfy a broad range of users, targets a specific group of users. For example, rather than writing a word processing package consider writing more specialised software to help freelance journalists keep track of their ideas, submissions and prospective editors. You will probably find this more specialised type of software easier to market and sell.

Fifteen ideas for your own software package

Consider writing:

1. Software for use at your place of work.

2. Software implementing your own specialist knowledge; for example, software which monitors the movement of companies shares or diagnoses faults in engines.

3. Enhancements and add-ons to existing top software products.

4. Software to fill gaps in your 'top twenty' most popular software products.

5. Specialist software for accountants, solicitors, journalists and so on.

6. Add-ons and **cheats** for popular computer games.

7. A computer game of your own.

8. Software which makes it easier for people to write or use other

software; for example, software which enables computer programmers to write their software more quickly and easily.

9. Communications software, enabling the use of modems and access to the Internet.

10. Software for the education market – schools and colleges – and any software which demonstrates how to complete or achieve a specific task.

11. Reference software: software which contains relatively unchanging information to which people might want to periodically refer, such as dictionaries, sporting and historical facts.

12. A software **utility**. This is a piece of software that allows users to complete a very specific action, like listing computer files or checking for computer viruses.

13. Software which enables people to draw, create or manipulate images.

14. Software that enhances people's enjoyment of their hobbies.

15. Software for any area as yet untouched by computers.

RUNNING YOUR OWN SOFTWARE BUSINESS

Whether you intend earning a full-time living or just making part-time extra income from your software, you will in effect be running a software business. People run their own businesses:

- to make a profit
- to have fun.

For your software business to survive, it must make a profit. If you enjoy your work at the same time then this enjoyment will be reflected in the quality of the product and service you offer. As a consequence, making a profit will be much easier.

Keeping records and accounts
Maintaining accurate business records and accounts has enormous benefits and need not be dull or boring.

Business records

- Help you control software development and work through ideas.

- Enable you to keep in touch with existing and potential customers.

- Show what customers have bought from you and at what price.

- Tell you what existing and potential customers intend to buy.

- Enable you to predict market trends and produce accurate sales forecasts.

Accounting records

- Show how profitable your business is.

- Show your major sources of business income and expenditure.

- Enable you to analyse your cash flow.

- Enable you to satisfy the requirements of the tax authorities.

Starting to keep records
Start keeping records now by noting the details of your software ideas. File them away neatly in an easily accessible location. Refer and add to them frequently. Note down any monies spent on equipment and any earnings from preliminary work. Without realising it you will soon start to build up a collection of indispensable notes, comments, facts and figures. These are the beginnings of your records and accounts system.

RESPECTING COPYRIGHT LAWS

An elementary understanding of **copyright** as it applies to software authors is necessary to ensure that you never become the subject of expensive legal action.

The meaning of copyright
Copyright means 'the right to copy'. Only *you* can publish your software, alter it, sell it and earn money from it. No one else has any

rights to publish, copy, change, or sell your software. It works the opposite way round too. You may not copy, change, publish, or sell other people's software.

Copyright law, changed from 1st July 1995, protects you and your software for your whole lifetime and a further 70 years (it used to be 50 years) after your death.

Copyright is your property, and as such can be sold or given to someone else. If this happens you relinquish your rights to the software and the buyer acquires all the rights you previously owned.

Establishing your copyright

Software is copyrighted from the moment you start writing it. There is no need to establish copyright, though software authors sometimes explicitly do this by displaying a copyright message similar to one below somewhere within their software:

Super Software Package © 1995 Your – Software Associates.

To prove beyond any reasonable doubt that you own the copyright to your software package, simply send a disk or disks containing your original program code to yourself by registered post. When you receive it, sign the receipt, making sure the date on the receipt is clear. Then deposit it in a safe place like a bank. Get a dated receipt from the bank too. This will be your ultimate protection in the event of a copyright dispute.

Copyrighting ideas

Although *ideas* for software packages cannot be copyrighted, the expression of the idea, in terms of how a software package is presented and used, is subject to copyright. This means for example that:

- an idea for a 'shoot 'em up' computer game cannot be copyrighted

- but creating a 'space invaders' lookalike, very similar to the original, is likely to infringe the original's author copyright.

CASE STUDIES

To illustrate some of the right and wrong ways of developing saleable software, you will meet three fictional software authors, all intending to make a living writing and selling their software. Each has a different blend of background and experience and will adopt their own personal approach to solving the problems they are presented with. Successive chapters will chart their progress and the consequences of the actions and decisions they take.

Dave Williams: young computer programmer

A young, talented, enthusiastic, but realistic individual who was determined to write a best-selling computer game, Dave had heard all the rags-to-riches stories, but was under no illusion about the size and complexity of his task. Although confident of his technical ability to write good software, he was particularly aware of his limited sales and marketing experience. Since leaving college he had been a permanent employee in the computing department of a large electrical retailer. Though confident, likeable and level-headed, Dave had no experience of running his own business and therefore planned to initially develop his software at home, using his own computer in his spare time.

Janette Morris: business woman

Previously successful in sales, Janette's latest job involved operating her employer's cumbersome, costly, half-computerised payroll system. With her solid commercial business experience Janette realised that there must be many small businesses with a real need for quality payroll software. Not only would this enable companies to more easily process their salaries and wage slips, it would also lead to real financial savings. Janette had written some software before, but not lately. Preparing carefully, her goal was to set up her own company supplying payroll software to small businesses.

Lance Armstrong: computer enthusiast and software guru

Lance believed that most of the software packages he had used were flawed in some way, and certainly costly to buy. He dreamt of using his much-vaunted technical ability to write his own software package, and felt that if this was offered at the right price people would naturally buy it and he would become rich. Lance was also inspired by the success achieved by an old school friend, now running his own small but successful software business, and reasoned that if his friend could do it then so could he.

Lance's idea was to produce the ultimate word processor, incorporating all the latest features and directly competing with the world's largest software companies. Working in his spare time at home, Lance considered his main strengths to be enthusiasm and technical ability, though readily admitted that he had yet to publish any of his own software, and that he had no experience of actually marketing and selling software.

DISCUSSION POINTS

1. Why do you want to develop and market your own software?

2. What in your view makes a software package popular?

3. What ideas do you have for a software package of your own?

2
Identifying Your Market

Once you have at least the beginnings of an idea for a software package, you can begin identifying and researching the market at which your idea is aimed. This will allow you to determine

- how saleable
- and how potentially profitable

your idea is.

Having a soundly based, saleable idea is vital. So before spending any further time or money, it is necessary to obtain a firm indication from the market itself that, after developing your software, you have a realistic chance of selling it and making a profit.

Ideas themselves cost nothing to begin with, but as the product develops costs can escalate quickly. This is particularly true when you start buying equipment and writing software in earnest. By identifying your own area of the market and then accurately researching it, you will ensure that costs and wasted effort are kept to a minimum.

Just what is the market and how does it work? More importantly, how do you find your place in it?

EXPLORING THE SOFTWARE MARKET

The software market is made up of software buyers and software sellers, both here and abroad. Buyers and sellers include:

- members of the public
- small businesses
- large companies
- central and local government.

Every possible kind of software is sold in this market, from the simplest of computer programs running on the smallest personal computers, to the most complex software running on the world's largest computers.

Competition within the market is fierce, with sellers constantly striving to promote the virtues and benefits of their own products over those of their competitors.

CHOOSING A MARKET AREA

Like all large markets, the software market is made up of a number of smaller market sectors, each consisting of buyers and sellers of specific, competing products. For example, the market for word processing software is a smaller market within the overall software market, and wholly separate from the computer games market. Before you can research your own market area, you must firstly identify it. This can be done in two main ways:

1. By identifying a specific group of people or business area, that your idea will benefit. For example, accountants, bakers, hospitals, oil and gas sectors. Specific markets like these are known as **vertical markets**.

2. By identifying a specific task that your idea will make easier for everyone, for example word processing software can be used by most people regardless of their profession or business area. Software of this type is often referred to as **mass market** software.

Writing vertical market software

If your idea is to provide software which handles the appointments system at your local doctor's surgery, then clearly the specific group of people to which your idea applies is doctors. Similarly, if your idea relates specifically to the petrochemical industry or to footwear manufacturers, then your idea is also aimed at a vertical market. Few people outside the intended vertical market have any use for such software, but this is of no importance at all, because right from the start the idea has been developed with a specialists audience in mind.

Vertical market customers might be:

- accountants
- athletes
- bakers
- computer programmers
- architects
- authors
- brewers
- doctors

- dentists
- estate agents
- gardeners
- linguists
- opticians
- solicitors
- engineers
- farmers
- landlords
- musicians
- pharmacists
- surveyors.

Vertical markets, being less competitive than mass markets, are often fertile ground for new software developers and have many advantages for those equipped to exploit them.

Advantages of writing and selling vertical market software

1. You know who your customers are (doctors, solicitors, accountants).

2. Consequently, it is easy to reach customers.

3. You can write software relevant specifically to your customers. There is no need to cater for anyone else.

4. You may already work within, or have knowledge of, the profession or business area that your customers work in.

5. As your software develops, so does your knowledge of your customers' business or interest areas. You become more able to talk knowledgeably to your customers, understand their needs and serve them better.

6. Market research is easy because the market is well defined.

7. Advertising your product is easy. Specialist magazines and trade journals can carry your adverts, and will often be prepared to review or feature your software.

8. Attending specialist trade exhibitions and conventions enables you to meet and talk to customers in one single location.

9. Vertical markets tend to be less competitive.

10. Buyers tend to become reliant on vertical market software and often remain loyal to an individual supplier for longer.

Disadvantages of writing and selling vertical market software

1. By definition there are fewer customers in a vertical market.

2. You are much more likely to be affected by a crisis or recession in your chosen market. For example, a recession in the housing market is likely to adversely affect sales of software to estate agents.

3. It can be difficult and expensive to obtain specialist information about an individual profession or business area if you do not already have it.

4. Vertical market buyers tend to buy from suppliers specialising in the same market area as they do.

5. A change in the law or the regulations that apply to your business area may render all of your software useless (this can also be an advantage, see chapter 9).

6. Vertical market buyers tend to have a wide range of different types of computer hardware. Many customers will be unable to run your software even if they wanted to.

7. Buyers may already be reliant on another supplier's software. It will therefore be much more difficult for them to justify buying your product.

8. Many vertical market customers have organised, well-established manual systems and often feel there is no need to automate them.

9. Certain vertical markets are very wary of computerising their businesses because of the associated risks.

10. It is possible that the group of people at which your software is aimed is slowly diminishing. For example, if your software controls the workload of traditional doorstep milkmen, then your market is gradually diminishing.

Writing mass market software

The most commonly seen software on the market today is mass market software – software that is used to complete a fairly specialised task, but which most people can use regardless of their profession or business area. The mass market attracts all the largest, best-known software companies, and everyone else too. All are eager to offer their products to buyers who, as a result, are presented with a wide selection of products to choose from.

For sellers, the mass market can be fiercely competitive and very difficult to break into for the first time. New software authors particularly find mass markets far more difficult to break into than vertical markets. However, with an excellent product, astute marketing and skilled, professional selling it is possible for the newcomer to make money in a mass market.

Ten examples of mass market software

word processors	spreadsheets
graphics software	hobby and leisure software
databases	personal finance software
games	operating systems
personal organisers	software utilities

The advantages of writing and selling mass market software correspond closely with the disadvantages of writing and selling vertical market software. Similarly, the disadvantages of the mass market are the main advantages of the vertical market.

Did you know?

1. UK customers buy around two million personal computers every year.

2. A fifth of all home users use their PCs solely for playing games.

3. Once written, a typical software package can be mass-produced by its author at a cost of under £10 per copy.

RESEARCHING YOUR MARKET

Having now decided the market sector you intend to write software for, the next step is to research that market. **Market research** is the process by which you attempt to derive the fullest and most accurate information about the market area you intend to compete in.

Researching the software market means determining:

• Who and how many customers there are, and where they can be reached.

• What interest, if any, these customers have in your idea.

• What, if any, computer hardware and software they currently use.

• The longevity of the market – how long it will last.

• Who and how many suppliers (competitors) there are.

• An estimation of your possible share of the financial value of the market.

All this information is readily available if you know where to look. Your task is to gather, isolate and summarise this information for your particular sector of the market. You can then use it to assess whether or not a viable market exists for your own intended software product.

Ten sources of software market information
Likely to be available cheaply and easily
1. Computer, industry and trade magazines, circulation figures, reader surveys, advertisements, reviews, customer interviews and company profiles.

2. Talking to potential customers: find out what interest they may have in your idea, and what computers and software they currently use.

3. Telephone directories show how many doctors, dentists, accountants, etc. exist in your area and how to contact them.

4. Television: current company and market news and information.

5. Newspapers: surveys, interviews, company and market news.

6. Books: detailed market information, statistics, outlook, and company profiles and historical data.

Likely to be more expensive or difficult to obtain

7. Specialist software market journals: detailed, up-to-the-minute market information.

8. Talking to software suppliers (your competitors).

9. Attending trade shows, exhibitions, and conventions.

10. Conducting market surveys.

Reducing costs

You will need to invest both time and money before you collect the earnings from your first software sale. Therefore, keeping in mind the need to reduce costs to a minimum, start to gather your market information from the sources numbers 1 to 6 in the above list. Resort to items 7 to 10 only if you really need to. Make detailed written notes of your findings and of any other relevant market information, keeping all notes clear and easily accessible. These notes will later become invaluable when you come to summarise market information.

Summarising market information

When all relevant market information has been gathered, the next step is to summarise it. This will present you with a clear, overall picture of your sector of the software market, and will enable you to decide, based on known market facts, whether or not the further development of your idea is likely to lead to a saleable and profitable software product.

Many methods can be used to summarise market information. Filling in the form shown in Figure 2 will help you to summarise the market information you have gathered and will enable you to make a personal assessment of your intended software market area.

Making up your mind

Once the form in Figure 2 is completed, notwithstanding any extra information you have yet to gather which is specific to your own idea, you will have most of what you need to make an informed decision about whether or not to proceed with your idea.

IS YOUR IDEA VIABLE AND SALEABLE?

Examine your completed form. Consider where you think the

		Example	**Actual**
a.	Who are your customers?	Garage owners	......
b.	What area of business are they in?	Vehicle servicing, retailing	......
c.	How many customers might have a general requirement for software *like* yours?	4,000	......
d.	How many potential customers at a. have you spoken to?	20	......
e.	What percentage of d. expressed a strong interest in your idea?	20%	......
f.	Use the percentage at e. to calculate how many people overall at c. are likely to want to buy your product.	800	......
g.	What makes of computer do the people at f. commonly use?	IBM Compatibles Personal computers	......
h.	Estimate the number of customers at f. who use the common types of computer at g.	600	......
i.	How many competitors directly compete in your market?	2 (Smithsons, Petrosoft)	......
j.	What customer benefits will distinguish your product from others?	Easy to use, cheap, more features	......
k.	For how many years will your software have applicability to your customers?	3	......
l.	What price do you initially expect to charge for your product (excl VAT)?	£100 per copy	......
m.	What annual charge will you make per customer per year for upgrades and telephone support?	£40	......
n.	Multiply l. by h. to give estimated sales.	£60,000	......
o.	Multiply m. by h. by k. to give total of upgrades/support fees.	£72,000	......
p.	Sum n. and o. and divide the result by k. to estimate your annual income.	£44,000	......
q.	Estimate your annual costs (account for special one-off costs like buying computers/hiring temporary staff).	£35,000	......
r.	Subtract q. from p. to leave an estimated annual profit/loss figure.	£9,000	......

Fig. 2. A software market profile.

34

problem areas are and how you might overcome them. Look particularly at your estimation of the size and longevity of your market, the interest level shown by potential customers in your product, and the number of competitors you have. Remember Figure 2 is a guide only. Starting any kind of business involves producing detailed cost breakdowns, sale/profit forecasts and business plans. (See Further Reading at the end of this book for sources of more detailed and specialised financial advice.)

Is your idea soundly based, well thought-out and researched, and is it saleable in enough numbers to make it profitable? It is now time to make a decision.

CHECKLIST

To help you reach a decision answer the following questions, being ruthlessly honest with yourself.

1. Are enough potential customers available and interested enough in your idea to make developing it a profitable proposition? (Depending on your product the practical minimum is 100-1000)   *Yes/No*

2. Are your potential customers easy to reach? (Can you readily contact them by, say, looking them up in a business telephone directory, or by advertising your product to them in a specialist magazine?)   *Yes/No*

3. Are your customers likely to have a need for your product over a number of months or years, rather than just once or for only a few weeks?   *Yes/No*

4. Are you sure that your software will still be up to date (with industry regulations/buying trends), and fully usable when you have finished developing it?   *Yes/No*

5. Are your potential customers currently using computers similar to that which you intend to develop your software on? If not will they be willing to switch or buy new computers specifically to run your software?   *Yes/No*

6. Will your product distinguish itself in terms of quality, presentation and ease of use from those of your competitors?   *Yes/No*

7. Can you sell software as well as being able to write it?   *Yes/No*

8. Can you readily identify the benefits of your software over those of your competitors?   *Yes/No*

9. Will the benefits of your software be easily demonstrable to customers?   *Yes/No*

10. Given the number and size of your competitors, can you still expect to make a profit selling your software?   *Yes/No*

11. Will your product be relatively cheap to develop?   *Yes/No*

12. Will your customers still exist when your product is ready for sale?   *Yes/No*

13. Is your estimation of the financial value of your market really accurate and, if so, is that value enough to enable you to recoup the cost of developing your product?   *Yes/No*

14. Are you motivated to both develop and, more importantly, sell your product?   *Yes/No*

15. Are you prepared to do most of the work yourself or employ others to do so where you do not have the necessary skills?   *Yes/No*

16. Is your idea viable and saleable?   *Yes/No*

If you have answered 'Yes' to every question then your idea probably has a good chance of being developed and sold as a software package. If you have answered 'No' to any one question, then think again. It is much less costly to drop your current idea than to develop it and later find that nobody wants it. You still have the option of exploring new ideas.

CASE STUDIES

Dave researches the games market

Dave's idea was to create a mass market computer game which involves one or more players scoring points while journeying through a three-dimensional jungle landscape, encountering fierce and friendly animals. Determined to research his market, Dave spoke to friends and members of several computer games clubs to test his idea, and was encouraged by the response. Dave knew that all club members read at least one monthly computer games magazine, and by looking at the magazines' circulation figures he estimated that he had a potential market of around half a million people – mostly young males owning small personal computers. From reader surveys, Dave noted that a typical software game had a life span of approximately 18 months and sold for around £30. Knowing the games market to be very competitive, Dave estimated that if only 0.5 per cent of all magazine readers bought his game his total revenue would be £75,000. Surprised by this, Dave decided to proceed further – but carefully.

Janette is sure of her facts

Janette's idea was to produce payroll software for small businesses and, after talking with several colleagues at a small business conference, Janette realised that her initial idea might have substantial merit. From conference handouts she assessed that her own customers would be small businesses employing up to 150 people, representing over ninety-eight per cent of the total number of companies in the UK – all with an on-going requirement for payroll software. By scanning newspapers, trade journals and speaking with small business advisors, she discovered that over fifty per cent of all small businesses were not yet computerised and the ones that were operated a complete mixture of computer systems. With two well-established competitors, Janette calculated that if she only won a 2.5 per cent share of the payroll market worth £10 million per year, her annual earnings before costs would be £250,000.

Lance forges ahead

Lance felt that most people using computers would probably have a use for his new word processor. With 200 million personal computers in the world, Lance saw a potential market of 200 million customers. He accepted that the five top selling word processors controlled ninety-five per cent of the market and a further one hundred different word processors competed for the remaining five per cent. Despite this, Lance was critical of the word processor he owned, at that time the number two best-seller, and resolved to improve on it by producing his own offering. An improvement on the world's number two best-seller would surely make his product the number one. Lance pondered over the logistical task of producing so many copies of his software, but otherwise felt that he had it all under control.

DISCUSSION POINTS

1. Your old business studies teacher asks about your future plans. You mention that you have a promising idea to develop a computer software package for sale. He is impressed, but asks what market research you intend to carry out to support your idea. What do you tell him?

2. A friend tells you of his idea to write a software package, designed to teach primary school children basic arithmetic. He would like to sell it to boost the income he gets from his full-time job. He gives no further details but asks whether you think his idea is feasible. What is your advice?

3. After researching the market, you have estimated that your idea is worth £40,000 per year, in a declining market, for the next three years. Bearing in mind that you have yet to start even writing the software, is your idea viable?

3
Defining Your Software Package

You now know whether your software idea is at least capable of being profitable. If it is not, return to chapter 1 and consider another idea.

The next step is to visualise how your software product will look when it is finished. To do this your product's name, its image, its list of features and its likely benefits to customers all need to be thought of and clarified. Visualising a finished product is useful for three reasons:

1. It will enable you to stimulate customer interest by referring to a 'real' product with a real name, an identity and a feature list.

2. It will further motivate you to develop and sell it.

3. A firm picture of your finished product with all of its features will help estimate how long such a product will take to develop.

IDENTIFYING THE TYPICAL CUSTOMER

To ensure maximum sales of your software package, it must appeal to as many of your customers as possible. It must:

- be visually attractive

- be seen by customers as a cast-iron solution to their problem

- project a professional image

- be perceived to represent good value for money.

The best way to ensure your product appeals to the highest possible number of customers is to create a profile of your 'typical' customer, then visualise how your product needs to look in order to appeal directly to them. This means conceiving an imaginary customer whose age, sex, background and character traits typify the kind of person most likely to buy your product. For example, in the case study of Dave Williams at the end of chapter 2 Dave reckons that a typical customer of his computer game is young, male, frequently reads games magazines, and occasionally attends computer clubs. After further thought Dave has refined and added to the profile of his typical customer, who he now believes:

- is a young male between 14–25 of varying background, education and social group

- owns a personal computer with at least five different computer games

- typically spends up to £30 on each game from money received from parents or earned from some kind of employment

- is an avid computer games player, up-to-date with and eager to acquire the latest computer games software

- is wary of the inferior products made to look good by glossy advertising, and tends to buy games only after having played a demonstration version of it at least three times.

Dave needs to visualise his game as being appealing to a customer fitting this description. You should attempt to do the same for your software package. Write down what you consider to be a profile of your typical customer, taking account of:

- age
- sex
- educational and social background
- employment
- sources of income
- general outlook
- the kind of computer owned (if any).

Now all you need to do is to create an image of your product that would appeal to your typical customer. Start by thinking of a suitable product name.

GIVING YOUR PRODUCT A NAME

Customers remember product names. The name of your software package is its identity and is crucial to its success. Like the name of any other product, the name of your software package should give an indication of what it is intended to be used for or who might typically use it.

For example, popular chess playing computer programs have names like Master Chess, Chess Genius, Chess Expert and Chess Champion. All these names are likely to be familiar to chess-playing customers, and give no room for doubt as to what the software is intended for. As a bonus, all these names also add to customer appeal by inferring that the software programs themselves play an excellent game of chess.

Even at this early stage, a good product name is essential. You have the option of changing the name later, but by associating a name with your product now you will be better able to plant the image of your product in customers' minds. It will also give your project as a whole an identity and will in itself be a motivating experience.

How a good product name helps
When considering a name for your product remember that good product names:

* give some indication of the product's intended use and/or intended audience

* are striking in some way, and therefore easily memorable

* are easily distinguishable from the names of competitors' products

* infer quality, ease of use, or some other positive attribute.

Dave Williams has provisionally named his product Adventures in Jungleland. This indicates that his software package is a game. The title is quite striking, memorable, unique and infers the excitement all games players are seeking.

Did you know?
1. Over a half of all features in modern software packages never get used.

Fig. 3. Example of a finished software product.

2. Almost all new software authors fail to talk to their customers before starting to write their software.

3. Around one in ten British households now own at least one personal computer.

VISUALISING THE FINISHED PRODUCT

The product name is important, but only one part in the overall image you want to convey to customers. Now try to visualise some other attributes of your product.

Looking good

Picture your finished product on a display shelf inside a computer shop, at the moment your typical customer walks in. The customer spots your product on the shelf. What does he see? What does your product look like? Is it packaged inside a box or in an envelope? If in a box, what size is the box and what is printed on it? What features and benefits are contained within your software and how are these illustrated on the packaging? How many software manuals will there be inside the box and what will they look like? What image will the product as a whole present to customers?

The customer then picks your product off the shelf, and is reading the notes on the packaging. Ask yourself whether your vision of the completed software package is attractive enough under closer scrutiny to tempt your typical customer into buying it.

Considering technical issues

The customer is now definitely interested in your software. He perceives an image of quality from the attractive, informative packaging and, after further study, he believes that your software will be eminently suitable for his needs.

The customer's next concern will be to ensure that his own computer has at least the minimum amount of **memory**, **disk space** and **processing power** (the **minimum specification**) needed to run your software. He also is interested to see whether or not your software is able to take advantage of any extra components that he might have added to his computer system – extra **memory**, a **sound card**, **speakers**, a **high resolution video card**, a **mouse**, and possibly a **printer**.

With all this in mind, think of the **type** and **specification** of the computer your typical customer owns. Your software package should be capable of running on a computer of this type and with this minimum specification. The customer will also expect to find this minimum specification printed somewhere on the packaging.

Complete the following checklist to obtain an indication of the minimum computer specification your software might need to be capable on running on.

Checklist

		Example	*Actual*
		(Dave Williams' Game)	
1.	Make of computer	IBM PC	....
2.	Minimum memory	2 Megabytes (Mb)	....
3.	Minimum disk space	4 Mb	....
4.	Video cards supported	VGA/SVGA	....
5.	Processor	80386 + later	....
6.	Operating system software	Windows 95	....
		MS-DOS 5.0	....
7.	Can your software be used by more than one person (on a network) at the same time?	No	....
8.	If yes then what networks	N/A	....
9.	Extra supported components:		
	sound cards and speakers	All popular	....
	extra memory	Up to 32 Mb	....
	floppy disks	3.5 inch only	....
	CD-Rom support	Yes	....
	mouse supported	Yes	....
	joystick supported	Yes	....
	printers	None	....
	plotters	None	....
	modems	None	....
	scanners	None	....
10.	Will all the above still be current, usable, available and relevant at least a year after your software has been completed?	Yes	....

ESTIMATING TIME SCALES

You should now have some thoughts about the appearance, image and technical requirements of your product. You will have defined your typical customer and will have in mind a list of product features that might appeal to him. The next stage is to estimate how long it will take to develop these features into a saleable product.

Reliable estimates can be made a lot easier by breaking up your whole project into smaller phases and individually estimating each phase. A typical software product is developed in a number of phases:

- listing and analysis of requirements
- design
- software development
- testing
- documentation
- initial advertising and product launch.

By understanding what is required from each of the above phases it is possible to:

1. Estimate how long each phase will take.

2. Estimate how long the whole project will take.

Drawing up a requirements list

This means listing all the tasks that customers require your software to be able to complete from them. For example, in our case study Janette Morris intends to produce payroll software for small businesses. Her initial feelings are that her software must at least be capable of:

- calculating salaries and wages for up to 150 employees

- handling weekly, two-weekly, and monthly wage payments

- calculating employees' gross and net pay

- calculating employees' tax and national insurance (NI) payments

- printing wage slips

- generating reports for management including an end-of-year payroll summary report.

However, in order to make a more accurate and detailed requirements list, Janette felt she would need to spend around ten working days (two weeks) talking face-to-face with some of her potential customers to find out exactly what they wanted.

How long will you need to complete a detailed requirements list for your software package?

Design

This is the process by which software is conceived and modelled so that, when written, it is capable of performing all of the tasks on the requirements lists. The design process might range from drawing simple **flow diagrams** and **screen layouts** to creating complex **multi-level design models**. Whatever design method you intend to use, estimate the length of time you think might be necessary to complete it.

Janette estimated that her design phase would take around sixty days (twelve weeks), at the end of which she would have enough detailed design documents to start developing software.

Software development

This is the actual coding of software – the writing of computer programs, often the most enjoyable (and time-consuming) phase of the project and can often be difficult to estimate. However, a good rule of thumb says that writing the software will take between one and three times as long as the design phase. Your estimate should include all the time necessary to ensure that the program works as intended most (ninety-nine per cent) of the time.

Janette went a step further than this. She produced a more detailed estimate of her software development phase, estimating the time required to write the individual programs she thought would make up her software package as a whole:

Menu structures	10 days
Fifteen detailed input screens	30 days
Gross pay calculations	5 days
Tax/NI calculations	6 days
Three management summary reports	12 days
End-of-year employee forms/reports	10 days
Sub total	73 days
10% contingency	7 days
Total	80 days

Janette wisely included extra days into her estimate just in case one or more of her programs took a little more time than she had expected.

Testing

Once written, programs need to be tested to ensure that they work properly, not just most of the time, but all of the time and for everyone. Testing programs means attempting to find circumstances and situations that could occur whilst the software is in use, which would cause the software to **crash**, **freeze** or generally display errors.

Janette knew that ease of use, consistency and above all accuracy were critical to the success of her payroll software. She knew that her customers would not tolerate even the smallest error when calculating their employees' wage payments and tax liabilities. Accordingly, she felt that her testing phase should be at least as long as her development phase, and therefore estimated that it would take seventy-nine days.

Documentation

This means producing **printed manuals** and developing **on-line (screen-based) help.** Typically, documentation includes information on:

- installing the software
- using the software
- solving common problems.

For her payroll system, Janette estimated:

1 Production of a user manual	25 days
2 Production of on-line help	15 days
3 Other documentation	10 days
Sub total	50 days
4 10% contingency	5 days
Total	55 days

Initial advertising and product launch

This phase often runs concurrently with the latter stages of the testing or documentation phases, but nevertheless requires estimating separately.

Consider what adverts and press releases you may need to prepare. Also consider the length of time that might be required to copy disks, print and bind manuals and to package them all up in a box. You may also need to estimate time for attending customer sites or trade shows during the launch phase of your project.

Janette initially allowed five days for the preparation of adverts, three days for press releases, two days for packaging, and a further seven days for visiting customers and attending trade shows: seventeen days in all.

Totalling it up

Total up the individual estimates for each phase of your project to get an indication of how long your software package as a whole will take to develop. This overall estimate is also the minimum number of working days that will elapse before your product can be launched and your first sale can be made.

Janette's overall estimate looked like this:

Requirements list	10 days
Design	60 days
Software development	79 days
Testing	79 days
Documentation	55 days
Initial advertising and product launch	17 days
Total	300 days

CASE STUDIES

Dave visualises his jungle adventure

Dave saw his game in three-dimensional colour graphics with fast **scrolling action** and lots of battling with ferocious jungle animals, before the player would finally reach the golden temple to collect the magnificent riches awaiting here. Dave envisaged his product being sold in a small oblong box, displaying Adventures in Jungleland in red and yellow fiery letters set on top of a fantasy jungle scene. Game features, and a list of compatible computers and supported components, would be displayed in gold and black on a white background on the edge of the box. Dave thought he himself represented the typical customer for his game, and also felt that his own computer's specification was close to what most of his customers would own.

Dave estimated that his project would take up to 160 days to complete. Most of the time would be spent writing and testing his software, though five days would be spent talking to customers to finalise requirements and a further five would be spent designing the software. Dave felt that his game would only require a very small user manual.

Janette acts quickly to capture her market

Janette envisaged her software packaged in a shoe-box size, navy blue box, with black and white pictures of salary slips, payroll forms and bank notes surrounding the metallic gold letters of her product's name – Business Payroll Gold. Janette realised that if she was to complete the project entirely by herself, her total estimate of 300 working days actually represented around 430 days of elapsed time after weekends and bank holidays were taken into account. Her main fear was that if she did not act swiftly to capture her market customers would adopt, and quickly become reliant upon, a competitor's product. Also, mindful of her dated technical skills, she decided it would be a good idea to employ the services of one or more computer programmers on a temporary basis, to help her produce the completed product in around 100 working days.

Lance predicts good times ahead

Lance saw his word processor – Buzz Word – as a combination of the existing top five word processors on the market, with all their faults removed and resplendent with all the extra features he himself had always wanted in a word processor. Lance felt that customers would automatically buy his product when they saw how impressive it was. He also felt that packaging and presentation were merely details and should not concern him until later.

Lance thought that requirements and product design could be completed in a very short time, that programming was most likely to take quite some time and testing would be easy, but made no real attempts to estimate his project properly. Lance also intended to write his software manuals as he went and had also made up his mind to advertise his software primarily in computer magazines.

DISCUSSION POINTS

1. How do you visualise your finished software product?
2. How long do you estimate your product will take to develop, and how did you arrive at this estimate?
3. For various reasons most software projects tend to take longer to complete than initially forecast. Do you feel that your estimate is accurate and have you included any extra days as a contingency measure?

4
Developing a Marketing Plan

Now that you have some idea of the computer your software will run on, what features it will contain and an approximate software launch date, the next stage is to develop a marketing plan. This will show you how best to bring your product to market by ensuring that your software:

- does exactly what your customers want it to

- is realistically priced

- is effectively advertised

- is packaged sensibly and attractively

- is effectively distributed to customers.

MEETING POTENTIAL CUSTOMERS

In a competitive market, with many similar products on offer, customers are able to choose the product they feel best suits their individual needs. Therefore, to sell your software it is essential to know as much about your potential customers and their needs as possible.

You already know who your typical customer is, where they live, their business and interests. Start by asking yourself who you know or can contact that closely resembles your typical customer. Look among:

- friends
- relations
- work colleagues

- fellow club members
- fellow sports players
- local businesses.

Getting advice

When you have identified a few representative people, give one or two of them a call. Explain your purpose and ask if they would mind meeting you to talk over your software idea. Perhaps, as specialists, they could also offer you some advice. Most people are only too willing to offer help and advice to those who ask properly and courteously for it.

Remember that your aim is to develop a marketing plan. When you meet be polite, but restrict the conversation, as far as possible, to their needs and requirements as customers, their preferences and wishes, and how these can best be met by your software package. Try to derive as much information as possible from your meeting, specifically including what they as customers feel is a:

- list of features the software must include at a minimum

- list of desirable features

- reasonable price for software which has these capabilities

- suitable place to advertise the software

- suitable place to go to buy this kind of software.

BUILDING A CUSTOMER WISH LIST

A customer wish list, in this context, is a list of features and capabilities that the customer wishes to see incorporated into your software package. Customer wish lists combine to become your requirements list. Meeting and speaking with a few potential customers will quickly enable you to build quite a sizeable requirements list.

Formalising requirements

The next stage is to develop your initial findings into a full, complete set of customer requirements, ordered in some way and presented logically. The completed requirements list will then become the principal document from which your software package is designed.

Consider the requirements list you have assembled so far. Ask yourself:

- How many requirements have you listed?

- Is the list complete?

- Are the requirements listed in a logical order?

- Is the requirements list well presented and easy to read?

There is no general rule which says how many entries there should be on a requirements list. It simply depends on the type and complexity of the software package under development. However, a typical requirements list for an average software package under development by an individual or small software company might have between thirty and 300 requirements.

Adding your own requirements

Your requirements list should contain all of the requirements your software package is intended to satisfy, and should be complete in all respects before proceeding with the design phase of your product. If it is not complete, it is possible your software could be designed omitting important details. It is perfectly proper for you to add further or residual requirements to your list if they are missing.

The following guidelines will help you ensure that your requirements list is as complete as possible.

1. Note any requirements that you know the customer must have but which have not been mentioned yet.

2. Note any of your own ideas which would lead to further efficiencies in your typical customer's working methods.

3. Examine the products of your competitors. List any features they provide which you have not yet listed as requirements.

Ordering your requirements list

For easy reference your requirements should be numbered and ordered in a logical way. For example, it is common to list requirements in order of importance, with the most important requirements listed first.

It is also common to group related requirements together. This means, for example, listing all requirements related to accessing and using printers together, separated from other groups of requirements.

Presenting the completed requirements list

The completed requirements list can be presented in many ways. Janette Morris chose a commonly used format for hers. Here is a small extract.

Business Payroll Gold (BPG) requirements list

1.	Section One	(mandatory requirements)	34 total
2.	Section Two	(highly desirable but not essential)	25 total
3.	Section Three	(desirable)	15 total
4.	Section Four	(others)	23 total
			97 total

Page 1
Section One (mandatory requirements)

Requirement Number	Category	Description
1.	Hardware	BPG shall be capable of running on any IBM compatible personal computer (PC) with at least 4Mb Memory/60Mb disk and an 80386 25 Mhz processor.
2.	Hardware	BPG shall be capable of running on a network of PCs.
3.	Hardware	BPG shall be capable of displaying text output to all screen types (MDA/EGA/VGA/SVGA) and so on.
. . . .		
17.	Printer	BPG shall be capable of printing output to all IBM and Epson compatible printers, dot matrix and laser printers.
18.	Printer	BPG shall be capable of printing multiple copies of any printed output.
19.	Printer	BPG shall be capable of detecting that a required printer is switched off, out of paper, or otherwise not in use and issuing an appropriate warning.

. . . .

| 23. | Payroll | BPG shall be capable of calculating gross pay, net pay, tax and NI payments for up to 150 different employees who may be paid weekly, two-weekly or monthly. |

LEARNING FROM COMPETITORS

Competition is a fact of life in the market place. However, rather than fear competitors you can learn from them.

It is likely that your established competitors are already following their own marketing plans. By studying their methods, and learning from their successes and failures, your own marketing plan will be a lot easier to develop. Consider your competitors, particularly:

● what products they sell

● how and where they advertise

● how they package their products

● what documentation they provide

● what prices they charge

● how they distribute (deliver) their products to customers

● how successful they are.

You can then assess the suitability of their methods and strategies, in each of the above categories, to your own intended product.

Developing software for different levels of user

Rather than providing a single software product for all customers, many companies provide **graduated levels** of the same product, each aimed at a specific level of customer or user. For instance, they might provide:

● A demonstration version of their software for customers wanting to try the product before buying it.

- A 'lite' version for customers whose needs can be satisfied with the basic facilities this kind of version supplies.

- A standard version for ordinary customers.

- A professional version for advanced users and the most demanding customers.

This results in excellent market coverage, from interested potential customers and newcomers to advanced users, with more or less the same product. Assess the suitability of this approach to your product.

Advertising your software

Effective advertising means teaching as many *applicable* customers as possible, with a clear, precise message at a minimum cost. Examine and list how and where your competitors advertise. It may be:

- in trade and specialist journals

- at trade shows, exhibitions

- by direct mail

- on the Internet and other on-line service providers

- by personally contacting customers

- in magazines, newspapers

- on television.

For each entry on the list consider carefully its applicability to your own idea and particularly to your own typical customer. Then use Figure 4 to form your advertising strategy.

How most small software companies advertise

Most small software companies prefer to advertise their products in specialist trade magazines, trade journals and computer magazines. The customers they need to reach are often employed or engaged in some form of specialist activity, and it makes sense to advertise in publications that are produced especially for them.

For the same reasons, many also attend and advertise their

1. **Trade magazines/journals**

   Title　　　　　　　Circulation　　　　　Weekly/Monthly

   _____　_____　_____

   _____　_____　_____

   _____　_____　_____

2. **Trade shows and exhibitions**

   Trade show name　Venue　　Frequency　　　Dates

   _____　_____　_____　_____

   _____　_____　_____　_____

3. **Mail shots** Yes/No　　If yes approximate frequency

4. **On-line services** (bulletin boards, the Internet)　Yes/No
   If yes which on-line services will you use?_____

5. Personally contacting customers by telephone　Yes/No
   If yes how will you know who to contact?_____

6　Non-trade magazines, newspapers

   Title　　　　　　　Circulation　　　　　Weekly/Monthly

   _____　_____　_____

   _____　_____　_____

   _____　_____　_____

7. Other

   _____

   _____

   _____

   _____

Fig. 4. Where will you advertise?

products at trade shows and exhibitions, where they can be sure of reaching high numbers of potential customers in a single location over a short time.

Some use direct mailing to target potential customers who, they feel, might be interested in their software, and an increasing number are waking up to the advertising potential of on-line mediums like the Internet.

There is still considerable customer resistance to telephone sales and advertising techniques, and general newspaper and TV advertising are either not appropriate or prohibitively expensive for most small software companies.

Planning to package your product

Most software nowadays is packaged in small oblong boxes made from stiff, hard-wearing cardboard material, sometimes shrink-wrapped inside a transparent plastic or polythene covering. Stiff-backed paper envelopes and plastic CD-ROM cases are also quite popular for packaging small numbers of disks and very small software manuals.

In general your packaging should be:

- Attractive, informative and well designed.

- Sturdy, resistant to buckling, tearing or breaking when in transit.

- Hard wearing and resilient to constant handling.

- A flat, regular shape, easy to store in quantity.

Planning to produce software manuals

People generally dislike and avoid reading software manuals. However, the same people would be appalled to receive a software package that contained no manuals at all.

Depending on the software product, customers typically expect at least:

- a **user guide**

- a **quick reference card**

- a **licence agreement form**.

The user guide is the main guide to which the user will refer in order to find out how to use the software or how to resolve software problems. It should be either:

- in paperback book form

- or contained as loose pages inside a hard ring-bound folder

- or sheets of high quality paper, folded and stapled at the middle (small manuals only).

The user guide should contain clear, readable print on good quality paper. The written content should be clear, concise, easy to read and no longer than absolutely necessary.

The quick reference card contains a brief, at a glance summary of the software's major features, commands and keystrokes.

Licence agreements spell out the legal terms and conditions under which you, the supplier, have supplied the software to the customer.

Did you know?

1. Around a third of all software development projects are cancelled before completion and over a half are completed late.

2. The main cost of developing a software package is time.

3. Businesses buy three times as much software as home users.

TESTING MARKET PRICE SENSITIVITY

In general, the price of a product is proportional to its level of sales. The lower the price the higher the sales and an increase in price usually leads to lower sales. The same is true for software products – but there are a few peculiar exceptions.

- Customers assume very cheap software is of very poor quality and therefore tend to be suspicious of it.

- Customers assume very expensive software must be excellent quality and are therefore attracted to it.

- Some customers will not buy software at any price until they have tried it out first. Once they have tried it and found it suitable they are often prepared to pay much more for it than they would otherwise have expected to.

Setting a provisional price

With the above in mind decide on a provisional price or price range for your software product. Look at the prices currently charged by your competitors and measure their products with the one you are about to start work on. Listen to what your customers have told you is a price they are prepared to pay. Then calculate a price at which, given your sales forecast and anticipated costs, will deliver you a profit. Remember that:

- A price of £49.99 is much more palatable than £50.00.

- If VAT is applicable then this must be included in your total price.

- Setting a slightly higher price for a quality product is entirely justified.

- 'Lite', standard and professional versions can be offered at graduated prices.

- Demonstration versions are usually free, or available at a nominal cost.

USING MAGAZINES, SHAREWARE VENDORS AND RETAILERS

All that remains to be completed in your marketing plan is your intended distribution method. In marketing terms, distributing your product means delivering it to customers. For software packages the following distribution methods are most commonly used:

- mail order (by post)
- shareware
- bulletin boards, the Internet, other on-line services
- computer magazine disks
- retailers
- Value Added Resellers (VARs).

Many small software companies use the mail order marketing channel in some way. This usually means supplying software by post to customers who have seen a magazine advertisement or mail shot letter and have ordered software by post or by telephone as a result.

Using shareware

Shareware is also a common means of distributing software nowadays. Software authors supply shareware vendors with a single copy of (usually) a demonstration version of their software. The vendor cannot sell the software itself, but is permitted to make unlimited copies of the software for distribution. The vendor makes a profit by charging shareware buyers for the media on which the software is supplied, its postage, packaging and handling, rather than for the software itself.

In this way the author achieves wide distribution for minimal outlay, and customers can try the demonstration copy of the software before deciding to buy the fully working version directly from the author.

Bulletin boards and the Internet

On-line services in general are rapidly becoming popular as a method for distributing software. The idea is similar to shareware but with no shareware vendor. Authors upload demonstration software on to a number of popular bulletin boards, or on to the shareware section of the Internet, and hope that the users of these on-line services will download the software in order to try it. If sufficiently impressed, they again are encouraged to buy the fully working version directly from the author.

Using computer magazines

Computer magazines often come with floppy disks or CD-ROM disks taped to the front cover. These cover disks frequently contain author's demonstration software and sometimes even fully working software. Magazine editors are continually searching for well presented and easy to use software, demonstration or otherwise, which they can include on their cover disks – it helps them to sell their magazines. For the author, a widely applicable audience is reached and potential sales of the fully fledged version are only a phone call away.

Using retailers

Software companies typically supply computer shops and stores with fully working, prepackaged software, at wholesale prices. After adding a mark-up retailers display and sell the software to the public. At present retailers tend only to stock the most popular software products, and breaking into the retail distribution sector can be difficult for new software authors.

Using Value Added Resellers (VARs)

VARs are retailers offering a more specialised service to customers. Software VARs are typically also experts in the software packages they sell. In addition to simply selling software products, they are also able to offer expert advice, training and support to their customers. New software authors will have to wait until their products are fully established before being able to use VARs as a distribution channel.

Your distribution method

Most small companies and individual software authors use a combination of mail order methods, shareware vendors, bulletin boards and occasionally magazine cover disks to distribute their products. New software authors are advised to follow suit. Later, when your software becomes more popular and well known, it will be easier to persuade retailers and VARs to stock it.

CASE STUDIES

Dave forms a marketing plan

To fill his requirements list Dave spoke with fifteen members of his computer club. From these conversations and a study of five leading adventure games, Dave prepared a full and detailed requirements list. He planned to advertise mainly in games magazines, just as his competitors did, and to use bulletin boards, shareware vendors and magazine cover disks to distribute a demonstration version of his game, which he hoped would tempt users into buying the full version for a provisional price of £29.99. Dave intended to supply his software on a single floppy disk, accompanied by one small glossy manual, a licence agreement and a post-paid registration card, all housed inside a stiff cardboard box, roughly the same size and shape as a small hardback book.

Janette talks to small businesses

Janette contacted four former business colleagues, all of whom were now proprietors of their own small businesses, to talk over her payroll idea. Between them they gave Janette many requirements for her list, which she completed after undertaking a full study of her own employer's payroll system. She decided the best way to initially advertise her product would be to mail-shot local businesses with small, carefully worded colour brochures detailing the features and benefits of her software. She also noticed two small business trade fairs and resolved to set up an advertising stand at each.

Janette decided to produce several versions of her product – a 'lite' version for businesses with less than twenty employees, a standard version for 20–150 employees, and a professional version for companies with over 150 employees, provisionally pricing them at £69.99, £199.99 and £399.99 respectively.

Lance sets his price

Lance completed his requirements list from a short study of his own word processor. Despite the relatively short time spent gathering requirements, Lance was very surprised at their number and complexity, but otherwise felt that his list was well ordered, well presented and entirely suitable for his needs.

Lance had bought his existing word processor from a local retailer after noticing an advert for it in a computer magazine. Accordingly, Lance felt that his best plan would be to place advertisements in the five highest selling computer magazines, and to use a combination of mail order methods and retailers to distribute his product. Eager to start writing software as soon as possible, Lance quickly set a provisional product price of £99.99 and started work immediately.

DISCUSSION POINTS

1. What do your typical customers require of your software package?

2. Who are your competitors and what can you learn from the way they advertise and distribute their products?

3. What do you consider to be a reasonable price for your software?

5
Writing Software

Now that your marketing plans are in place and your requirements list is full, software development can begin in earnest – at last! For many, the enjoyment of writing software wholly justifies the risk of not receiving any money for their work. However, for those with an eye on making a profit it is still necessary to ensure that the initial idea is turned into a profitable product. This can be achieved by:

- Drawing up project time scales and deadlines and sticking to them.

- Careful software design using the requirements list.

- Writing quality, easy-to-use software.

- Thorough software testing.

- Producing concise and clear documentation.

- Adequately protecting your software against unauthorised use.

PLANNING YOUR PROJECT

In chapter 3 you estimated time scales for the completion of each phase of your software project and by so doing were able to estimate an approximate product launch date. To ensure that this launch date is reached with a finished software product, it is necessary to derive completion dates for each remaining phase of the project – and to ensure you work within them. You need to know estimated completion dates for the project's:

- design phase

- software development

63

DAVE WILLIAMS		PROJECT PLAN		ADVENTURES IN JUNGLELAND		
PHASE	JAN	FEB	MARCH	APRIL	MAY	JUNE
GATHER REQUIREMENTS	1/1 – 15/1 → 15 DAYS					
DESIGN	16/1 – → 21 DAYS	5/2 ▶				
PROGRAMMING		6/2 →	– 75 DAYS	21/4 ▶		
TESTING				21/4 – 32 DAYS	– 23/5 ▶	
DOCUMENTATION					24/5 – 31/5 → 8 DAYS	
PACKAGING						1/6 – 5/6 ▶ 5 DAYS
LAUNCH!						(6/6) *

Fig. 5. Page from a software project plan.

- software testing

- documentation phase

- final preparation for launch.

By doing this you will be able to accurately monitor your progress towards the final launch date. If you finish one phase either earlier or later than estimated, you will immediately be able to calculate the effect of this on your product's final launch date.

Breaking down the project in this way means that you are effectively creating a project plan. Your project plan, at a very simple level, is a list of dates by which known tasks (project phases) should have been either started or completed.

Figure 5 is an example of a simple project plan. Using it as a guide, create a project plan for your own project. If you need to, lay your project plan out in a different way; just make sure that each task of each phase is listed and that you can clearly see its start and end dates, and duration.

DESIGNING YOUR SOFTWARE

Software design is driven by the requirements list. The design process itself, which may be carried out many different ways, should result in a number of **documents, paper models** and **program specifications**, from which the software itself can be written directly. It is recommended that each requirement is examined in turn and individual standards drawn up for designing:

- how the software will look and be used on screen

- data storage and access

- processing logic and calculations.

Designing screens and menus
Customers will judge the quality of your software package largely on what it looks like on screen and how easy it is to operate. It is therefore essential that common standards are developed and implemented governing such things as:

- **screen layouts**

- **screen colours**

- **menu structures**

- **keyboard** and **optional mouse** functionality.

Screen layouts
These need to be standard across the whole software package. Users will become confused otherwise. A good idea is to create a **template screen** with a typical layout, get it exactly as you want it then base all other screen layouts on it.

Screen colours
Colours are important too. Use the same colour to denote similar features across many screens. Do not use colours which are too bright or which dazzle the eye, and only use flashing colours to emphasise the occurrence of unusual conditions, such as errors. Also remember that some users may use mono (black and white) screens, so ensure your colour scheme works for them too.

Menu structures
Menu structures should be logically ordered and easy to access. Typically, top-level menus provide access to generalised operations like Reports, whereas further down the menu structure there are likely to be menu options providing access to more specific operations like Monthly Payroll Report. Menus can be displayed in fixed positions, in a 'ring' design horizontally spread across the top or bottom line of the screen, or in a 'pop up' or 'pull down' fashion where the user typically clicks the mouse button over the top of a menu title and the whole menu appears.

Keyboard and optional mouse functionality
Where specific keys or mouse actions are defined they should be common across the whole software package. For instance, if you plan to use the F1 keyboard function key to allow users to access on-line help, ensure that this key is always used for this purpose.

Writing standard data access routines

Consider Janette's payroll software. Different screens in her package will need to access employee information, tax and National Insurance tables – all held as data on her computer's disk. It would be silly for Janette to write individual data access routines for each of her fifteen main screens. Instead, she ought to write one standard routine which reads data from disk, and one which writes data to disk. These standard routines can then be called by any of her fifteen screens needing to read or write such data. This approach would eliminate program code duplication and as a result make the testing phase of her project a lot easier.

Standardising calculations

Logic and program calculations are more difficult to standardise. However, in Janette's case her software may need to calculate gross and net pay on a number of different screens. For consistency, accuracy and to again avoid duplication of effort, Janette's best course would be to design a single software routine capable of performing these calculations and allow it to be called from any screen needing gross or net pay calculations to be performed.

WRITING SOFTWARE

The creation of quality software demands a high level of technical skill and can progress in any number of ways. The following questions and answers will illustrate some of the facts software authors frequently ask for as they begin writing software.

What type of computer shall I write my software on?
The computer owned by your typical customer with its minimum specification (see chapter 3).

What computer language shall I write my software in?
This depends on your product. However, the following gives a general guide to popular languages and the type of software professional software authors use them for.

Computer language	Ideal for writing
Assembly language (assembler)	Games, operating systems, device drivers and any software where speed is critical or where a very high level of control of the computer is required.
C/C+ +	Games, operating systems, word processors, spreadsheets, graphics programs, communications programs, most complex software.

Pascal	Most home or business software, though not commonly used for games or operating systems.
BASIC	Most home or business software, though not commonly used for games, operating systems or any programs where speed of operation is critical.
4GL (forth generation languages)	Business or home software which requires easy access to a complex database to retrieve structured information.
Fortran	Scientific or engineering-type software where the emphasis is on the need to perform highly complex mathematical or scientific calculations.
Prolog, lisp	Artificial intelligence software and any software that uses expert knowledge to solve a particular problem.

My software package is likely to be large and complex. How do I start writing it?
Again this depends on the nature of your individual software package. Many professional software authors develop software as follows:

• Menus structures first. Once in place, navigation around the whole product will be easy.

• Next a basic, representative screen is chosen and is coded so that the author can assess and fine-tune its colours scheme, appearance and ease of operation. Once completed this screen can be adopted as a standard and can also be used as a template on which to base other screens.

• Next to be coded are all commonly used routines handling such activities as database storage and retrieval, printer access, standard calculations and any routines likely to be called by more than one screen.

• Remaining screens are coded in full, using a template screen as a standard and calling the common outlines just written.

- Software which operates other less commonly used peripherals like modems, scanners and plotters is coded next.

- With a more or less finished product, the last step usually completed is to develop an on-line help system.

How can I ensure that the software I have written will appeal to my customers?
Implicit in your design are all your customers' requirements. The software itself, if correctly designed, will do all that your customers have asked it to do. All that you need to do is ensure that a typical customer finds your software attractive, intuitive and easy to use. The best way to do this is to ask a few of the people you spoke to at the requirements stage to come along and have a look at the software you have produced and to give their comments.

Is it necessary to copy my software in case a disaster happens and I lose all my work?
Yes, you must. At least once per day copy all your own software, and any other software of which you do not have an up-to-date copy, on to separate floppy disks or magnetic tape. These copies, known as **back up** or security copies, should be stored in a safe location well away from your computer. In the event of disaster and loss of software, these security copies can be retrieved and your software copied back on to your computer.

Did you know?
1. Over a half of all home software has been copied illegally.

2. Testing software can take up to three times as long as writing it.

3. Some business software packages running on large mainframe computers are supplied with over fifty different manuals of instruction.

TESTING AND DOCUMENTING

Even top-selling software packages contain errors, or **bugs** as they are commonly known. Software bugs can cause customers (and you) many problems. Eliminating as many as possible from your own software is your next goal.

Ironing out software bugs

Though your software may appear to work properly most of the time, in reality there are probably circumstances and situations which will lead to it reacting in strange, inexplicable ways and possibly displaying incorrect information on the screen. You need to identify these situations and test to see how your software reacts to them. This can be done in a number of ways. Test the reaction of your software to:

- very high, very low and average values for numerical data

- lower and upper case words for alphabetical data

- large amounts of data

- small amounts of data

- rare and seldom used methods of operation

- external devices such as printers or modems which are not turned on or which are otherwise not operational

- retrieving corrupted data from the database

- important data being accessed by more than one person at the same time (if applicable).

If any unexpected bugs occur during your tests, then the software should be corrected and retested again to prove that

- the original bugs have been eliminated

- no new bugs have been introduced.

Using beta test sites

Another commonly used method of testing software is to freely distribute pre-release versions of your software to potential customers for them to test it. So-called **beta test users** will often be happy to get their hands on your new software early and in return will provide you with a list of problems they have found for you to fix.

This method results in more thorough and extensive testing than you could have otherwise achieved alone, and many of the beta testers will also become customers of your final version when it is ready.

Preparing final documentation

Documentation is usually one of the last tasks to be completed when developing a software package. The reason for this, people say, is that only when software development is completed are you fully aware of all its features and methods of operation. This is true to a certain extent, though some people argue that documentation can actually be produced a lot earlier, perhaps during the design phase, when all requirements, feature lists and methods of operation are known but before any software has actually been written.

Whenever it is initially prepared, both paper and on-line documentation need to be finalised to accompany the finished software to market. This means completing the user guide, a quick reference guide, a licence agreement and possibly other forms of documentation, including:

- a short tutorial guide to your product

- a registration card

- technical notes

- last-minute additions and changes to the user guide

- an errata sheet listing known misprints or errors.

When all this is completed, you can start to prepare your finalised software package for market.

PREPARING FOR MARKET

When your software is completed there are one or two more things to consider before you can officially launch it.

- A final product name and a version number.

- A final pricing policy.

- Final packaging details.

- A copy protection mechanism.

You may decide that your initial product name is still appropriate.

If you want to change it for any reason, now is the time to do it –
before the packaging is printed. You also need to assign a **version
number** to your software. This number will identify and distinguish
your initial software release from any subsequent releases whose
version numbers will probably be higher.

Normally the first release of a completed software package is
given a number of 1.00; the initial digit (1) shows that this is the first
major release of this software. A version of, say, 1.01 typically
indicates that the software is on its first major release but that a few
bugs have been fixed or extra features have been added, and a
version of 1.10 indicates that the software is on its first major release
but has been significantly revised since the initial release. A version
of 2.00 indicates that the software has probably been largely
redesigned or rewritten since the first major release.

Many software companies, however, introduce their software at,
say, version 1.5 or 2.1 or similar. This is a marketing ploy to make it
appear that their software package is more mature and established
than it actually is.

Setting a final price
Your final price should be fairly close to your provisional price.
Change it only if you feel your market has substantially changed
whilst you were developing your software, or otherwise feel that
your software is of substantially more or less value to customers
than you originally thought.

Protecting your software
Unfortunately, there are unscrupulous people who are only too
happy to copy your software and use it without paying for it. You
should seriously consider employing some methods of software
protection to guard against this – it could prevent you losing a
substantial sum of money in lost sales. Various software protection
methods are commonly used, including:

• Allocating serial numbers.

• Setting a maximum number of times software can be installed.

• Incorporating a password protection scheme.

• Using specialist copy protection software.

- Setting an expiry date within the software which renders it unusable after a certain length of time if it has not been registered.

- Using a software **dongle** – a piece of hardware which usually fits into a slot at the back of the computer which is required to be present before the software will run.

Whatever protection method you choose (if any), remember that copy protection mechanisms are only successful if they

- stop unauthorised use

- are difficult to circumvent or break

- do not penalise customers who legitimately paid for the software.

In our case study, Dave Williams adopted a clever approach to copy protection for his computer game. He built in some special software which detected whether or not the software was an original copy or an illegally duplicated copy. If the software was being used illegally, Dave arranged to 'switch' his game into demonstration mode. Since his real demonstration version was free anyway, he could only benefit from this and achieve a wider distribution for his game.

CASE STUDIES

Dave delivers quality software
Dave produced several paper drawings of his game's main characters, animals and scenic backgrounds and passed them to members of his computer club for their comments. He also wrote a small narrative covering the typical events that might occur during each phase of his game and checked these against his requirements list, to make sure he had included everything.

Dave's primary concern was to produce a game fast enough in operation to be playable by games experts and so chose assembly language to develop his software.

From his design Dave worked hard to design and write software to produce a standard game screen template, which he then used to create all his remaining screens. This made Dave's testing phase much easier and, as a result, he managed to deliver both a full and a demonstration version of his high quality, entertaining game in line with the time scales identified on his project plan.

Janette keeps to her project plan

Janette managed to complete her design on time, and then hired the services of two competent, professional programmers. After careful study the two programmers advised Janette to have her software developed in a flavour of BASIC suitable for creating business software. Janette agreed and set the programmers to work, carefully monitoring their progress, whilst she started writing the software manuals and other documentation. The two programmers performed well under her supervision, and both software development and testing were completed on time.

Janette decided that a **password** system would provide her software with adequate protection against unauthorised use.

Lance overruns his deadline

Programming initially in his favourite language Fortran, Lance soon realised that 'C' would have been a better choice, and decided to begin again. With few design documents in place, Lance was frustrated to find that he was continually wasting time backtracking to include missing features and to work around unexpected problems.

Lance's testing phase was also a nightmare, with numerous time-consuming bugs manifesting themselves throughout his software.

Lance struggled to write adequate documentation and finally finished his project a full eighteen months late. In the meantime, Lance was shocked to find that most of his main competitors had produced improved versions of their software, implementing new and useful features he had completely overlooked. Faced with having to curb his sales expectations he decided to drop his price from £99.99 to £39.99 in order to make his product attractive again.

DISCUSSION POINTS

1. How do you intended to design your software, and what design documents do you intend to produce that will ensure your software is developed in line with customer requirements?

2. What programming language do you intend to use to develop your software package and why have you chosen it?

3. How will you protect your software against illegal copying and other unauthorised use?

6
Launching Your Software

Now that your software has been written, the manuals completed and the packaging readied, you might think the major part of the effort of producing a saleable software package is over. In fact it has only just started. The key word in the last sentence is *saleable*. The technical work might be over (for the meantime) but the much more difficult task of selling software is just about to begin.

ANNOUNCING YOUR SOFTWARE

Selling your software begins in earnest by announcing it. This is normally achieved by

• writing and issuing press releases

• calling press conferences (larger software companies only).

The process of announcing a software package typically starts *long before* the software package is actually completed.

Producing a series of press releases
Press releases are notifications to the press (newspapers, magazines and so on) of particular newsworthy events. For example, a small software company might use press releases to notify various magazines and trade journals that a new software package is under development or is about to be released. The hope is that the magazines and journals selected to receive these press releases will find them of sufficient interest to publish them to their readership (potential buyers of the software), thereby providing the software company with 'free' publicity.

Since the cost of issuing press releases is relatively low when set against the prospect of free publicity, software companies normally prepare and issue press releases regularly and on an on-going basis.

This results in a series of press releases covering:

- pre-launch announcements

- a launch announcement

- post-launch announcements.

You might consider adopting the same approach. Depending on the length of your design and development phases, and the nature of your software package itself, start by preparing and submitting carefully worded press releases approximately seventy-five per cent of the way through your software development phase and continue to issue them on, say, a bi-monthly basis until your software is launched. After this you should continue to issue press releases on an even more frequent basis if possible.

Your pre-launch press releases might cover:

- An initial announcement that development work has begun.

- Further announcements giving more details of intended features.

- An announcement that the product is in beta test.

- An announcement of the final release date.

Each pre-release announcement should be designed to initiate and build a strong customer awareness of your software. Each should also serve to whet customers' appetites for your product, as the publicity bandwagon begins to gather momentum.

By the time the final release date is announced, the hope is that customer awareness and interest are heightened to such an extent that immediate sales are possible.

PRODUCING PRESS RELEASES AND ADVERTISEMENTS

The press release announcing your software's actual launch date should be prepared and issued during the latter stages of the beta testing phase of your project. This amounts to a virtual commitment on your part to release the software to customers on a specific date. Until now release dates should have been deliberately left vague, but this announcement should identify a specific date on which your software will be available for sale. All of the major features of your software, its uses and benefits, should also be incorporated into this press release, as should its price and an indication of the type of computer it is designed to run on. An example of a press release announcing the release of a software package is given in Figure 6.

Distributing press releases

Depending on the nature of their products, small software companies commonly prepare and distribute their press releases specifically for:

- customers' trade publications

- the computer trade press

- general computer magazines.

Build a publication list which you feel best covers the type of magazines and papers your typical customer reads. You need only prepare one press release, in terms of form and content, at a time. This single copy can then be duplicated and sent to the editors of the magazines you have selected. Address your press releases to the magazine editors, by name if possible, and well in advance of the magazine's publication date (up to six weeks in advance for weekly magazines, and up to three months in advance and sometimes longer for monthlies).

Though they are under no obligation to do so, most editors are happy to print details of new products likely to be of interest to their readers – it helps them fill space and sell more copies.

Getting your press release published

Editors often receive many more press releases than they can possibly print and therefore only publish the ones most likely to be of interest to their readers.

To give your press release the best chance of being published, ensure that

- it is attractively presented

- it is easy to read and relevant to both the editor and the readership

P
R
E
S
S

R
E
L
E
A
S
E

J.M. Software

Ref JM/96/11

Release Immediate   Date of Issue 01/11/9X

New Payroll Software
Cuts the Cost of Paying Staff

London, England – JM Software has announced its brand new payroll processing software package BUSINESS PAYROLL GOLD, designed to make it cheaper, easier and more cost effective for small businesses to pay the salaries and wages of their employees.

Able to handle weekly, fortnightly and monthly paid staff, BUSINESS PAYROLL GOLD quickly calculates employees' net salaries, Income Tax and National Insurance payments. Printed payslips can be produced for the entire workforce at the press of a button.

BUSINESS PAYROLL GOLD easily handles changes to salary levels, overtime payments, regular deductions from pay, alterations to personal tax codes and fully complies with current UK Income Tax and National Insurance regulations.

Janette Morris, founder of JM Software stated 'Business Payroll Gold is fully endorsed by the Small Business Confederation and comes in three versions for companies with up to 20, 150 and 500 employees. Prices are £69.99, £199.99 and £399.99 respectively'.

BUSINESS PAYROLL GOLD can run on any IBM compatible personal computer equipped with a hard disk and at least 1 Megabyte of memory and comes with networking capabilities as standard.

A free evaluation version of BUSINESS PAYROLL GOLD is available from JM Software, 11 Surbiton Way, London SW13 9RR. Tel: (0181) 434 4343.

—— ends ——

For further information please contact:
Janette Morris at J. M. Software
11 Surbiton Way, London SW13 9RR.
Tel: (0181) 434 4343
Fax: (0181) 434 4344

Fig. 6. A press release announcing a software package.

- it is easily distinguishable from all the other press releases on the editor's desk.

Never skimp on presentation. Editors rightly assume that shabby presentation is a reflection on the individual or company that produced it. Therefore always use quality bonded paper and ensure the print is clear and easily readable. The most important details should be emboldened or similarly emphasised. The title of the press release should be as interesting and startling as possible, to catch the editor's eye. Also make sure once the editor gets past reading the title, the content of the press release is interesting, informative and relevant enough to make him or her read to the end. Use '— end —' or '###' to denote the end of your press release.

Distinguishing your press release

Editors will notice, remember and be more likely to publish your press releases if you distinguish them in some way from all the others in the pile. For example,

- Use coloured paper rather than white.

- Use a distinctive letterhead design or company logo.

- Send the press release in a distinctive envelope.

- Include a photograph of yourself or a picture of your finished product.

However you distinguish your press release, remember that its distinguishing marks must be designed to enhance or support the image of overall professionalism and quality which you are trying to portray.

TARGETING CUSTOMERS

Press releases raise customer awareness and may lead to some interested readers contacting you in order to buy your software, but they do not usually result in a high number of sales. Surveys show that most smaller software company's sales come from:

- targeted advertising in specialist magazines

- carefully targeted mail shots

- trade shows.

Your first advertisement

To make sales, your press release campaign should be backed up with an effective advertising campaign. Effective advertising reaches the *maximum* number of appropriate people for a *minimum* cost.

Most smaller software companies advertise primarily in specialist magazines and trade journals, where costs are quite low and the readership highly appropriate to the software being offered. You might consider placing your first advert in the pages of such publications. You know which publications to advertise in – the ones your typical customer reads and the ones you have sent press releases to.

Mail shots

With mail shots you, the software supplier, prepare and distribute advertising material to customers through the post. Mail shots are an excellent way of targeting customers and can often lead to a respectable level of sales. Successful mail shots

- accurately target potential customers

- carry a clear, concise and attractive message

- are prepared at a minimum cost

- result in a customer response rate of over two per cent.

Successful mail shots

As with press releases, your mail shot advertising material should be clearly and attractively presented. For your initial mail shot, a list of potential customers should be prepared containing just those people who you have already contacted about your product, including

- friends

- business associates

- your typical customer(s)

- your beta test users

- anyone else who has expressed an interest in your product at any time.

Prepare the list carefully. Mail shots can be quite expensive and there is no point wasting money sending mail shot material to customers who are never likely to buy your software. Costs can be minimised by:

- Targeting customers extremely carefully.

- Producing cost-effective quantities of advertising material.

- Using second class post for mail shots of under fifty letters.

- Investigating discount postage schemes with the Post Office for higher quantities of mail.

Typical mail shot response rates vary in the range zero to two per cent. This means that if 100 adverts are posted out, then between none and two people will respond by sending an order for your software. This response rate may appear low to the newcomer. However, if costs are minimised a response rate of two per cent can be more than enough to be profitable.

Attending trade shows

Trade shows, conferences and exhibitions are also excellent places at which to advertise your software package – again because a large number of potential customers can be reached at a reasonable cost. Trade shows provide:

- a high concentration of customers in a single location at the same time

- an excellent opportunity for you to distribute your advertising material

- an excellent opportunity for you to demonstrate your software

- an excellent opportunity for you to talk face-to-face with customers.

SPREADING THE WORD

You need as many people as possible to know about your product's launch. As well as press releases, advertising, mail shots and trade shows, there are some other methods by which your new software product can be brought to the attention of a large number of people at a minimum cost:

- magazine reviews

- talks and demonstrations to user groups

- on-line advertising

- shareware vendors

- cover disks.

Writing magazine reviews

Unlike advertisements, magazine reviews cost you nothing in terms of what you pay to the magazine's publishers for printing them. Indeed, some magazine editors will even pay you for submitting a review!

Reviews are also likely to describe your product in far more detail than an advertisement ever could, and often take a more objective view of your software's applicability to the readership. Add to this the fact that most software product reviews take up considerably more page space than individual advertisements ever do, it can be seen that magazine reviews are an extremely cost-effective way of publicising your software to a large number of people. The problem lies in getting a review written and published. There are two principal ways of doing this.

1. Send free copies of your software to freelance writers and invite them to write a review of it for the magazines you have selected.

2. Write the review yourself.

Most specialised magazines rely heavily on the contributions made to them by freelance authors and reviewers. If you can get a copy of your software to them, persuading them that a written review is just the kind of thing an editor will pay them for, it is quite likely they will write and submit the review and that it will be published. The main problem is finding out who the freelance reviewers are and how to contact them. This can be done by:

- Studying recent copies of the magazine. Often contributor's names and some form of contact addresses are detailed at the end of the review.

- Building a list of freelance magazine contributors from contacts at trade shows, user groups and other face-to-face or telephone conversations.

- Calling the magazine's editor directly and asking for the names and addresses of all of the freelance reviewers of the magazine.

- Consulting one of the many specialised media directories detailing the names and addresses of freelance writers and reviewers. (For example, *Pims UK Media Directory* available from Pims House, 4 St Johns Place, London EC1M 4AH. Tel: (0171) 250 0870.)

You could consider writing and submitting the review yourself. Magazine editors do not necessarily use the same freelance contributors all the time, and are usually more interested in publishing quality reviews and articles with direct applicability to their readership than they are in remaining loyal to individual freelance contributors. Some editors may even pay you for your trouble!

Giving talks and demonstrations
To advertise your software you could also consider giving talks and demonstrations to the user groups, clubs and associations likely to be attended by potential customers of your product. Finding these groups and clubs need not be difficult. They will probably be

- listed in the specialised publications you intend to advertise in or submit reviews for

- obtainable by talking to your typical customers

- obtainable by talking to your beta test users

- obtainable through talking face-to-face with customers at trade shows and exhibitions.

If approached in the correct manner, many user groups and clubs will consider a visit from a software supplier like yourself to be an honour, and a chance for them to listen, talk about and view a product of interest to them in the company of a real 'expert'.

Did you know?

1. Popular newspapers can receive up to 1000 press releases daily – even trade magazines can receive 50–100 per week.

2. Most large software packages contain bugs.

3. Many fully operational software packages are given away free. Where? Mostly on PC magazine cover disks.

DISTRIBUTING YOUR SOFTWARE PACKAGE

Your product can also be brought to the attention of potential customers by distributing it to them so that they can try it out for themselves. This usually means creating a demonstration version of your software and distributing it to potential customers via

• bulletin boards, the Internet and other on-line services

• shareware vendors

• magazine cover disks.

To ensure your demonstration software is distributed in the volumes that you desire, it is necessary to place yourself in the position of the person likely to receive and distribute your demonstration version to potential customers.

This means that for bulletin board operators (**sysops**), a demonstration copy of your software should be easy to load, be accompanied with a short, interesting description of the product itself, and be accessible enough to potential users of bulletin board services to encourage them to download it to their own computers.

For shareware vendors your product should again be easily identifiable and easy to duplicate. The accompanying documentation should be short, concise and interesting enough to make the shareware vendor feel that your product is likely to be demanded in volume by shareware customers.

For computer magazine cover disks or CD-ROMs, the emphasis must be on the quality of the product itself. Editors of magazine cover disks generally only consider publishing software that is:

- of startlingly high quality

- applicable to a large proportion of its readership

- able to be physically contained on the single floppy disk or CD-ROM that usually accompanies the magazine.

CASE STUDIES

Dave announces his game early

Dave was acutely aware that his technical skills alone would not guarantee sales. Midway through his software development phase, he prepared and issued the first in a series of press releases, advertisements and reviews aimed at a list of publications specialising in reporting on leading-edge games software – the magazines Dave's typical customers would read. Dave also arranged to demonstrate his new software at several local computer games clubs, and also drew up a list of bulletin boards, shareware vendors and cover disk editors to which he would soon send demonstration copies of his software for distribution.

Dave's meticulous preparation paid off. Several publications carried the main details of his press releases and two even published full reviews of his new game, accompanied by a copy of his demonstration software on their cover disk. All in all a pleasing start, considering Dave's otherwise limited marketing and sales knowledge.

Janette successfully reaches many customers

Janette announced her payroll software well before it was actually ready for sale. Preparing a series of press releases, and issuing them to a number of selected magazines, she found that a good proportion of them actually found their way into print. Janette also contacted a freelance writer to explore the possibility of having a review written for a suitable magazine. This action paid dividends and many of Janette's potential customers noticed the review and contacted her to arrange product demonstrations.

Janette also prepared a select list of beta test users, local small businesses and other businesses which she knew were having problems with their existing payroll software. Her intention was to mail them with details of her own product. At a special reduced rate of postage she contacted 300 potential customers, and was surprised to receive over twenty requests for further information and eight firm orders for her new software – easily making her first mail shot a profitable one. Janette also set up a stand at a one-day trade show. Although no sales were made Janette achieved her main goal of distributing all of her advertising material to potential customers.

Lance finds difficulty in placing his adverts

Because of program bugs and technical problems resulting in extended software development and testing phases, Lance had little time to prepare press releases and advertising material. Consequently what he did manage to produce was rushed and by his own admission not up to standard. As a result, few magazines actually published any details of Lance's press releases.

Lance also found that the adverts he had intended to place could not be placed in the appropriate editions because they had missed important magazine copy dates. Ironically, Lance thought that his word processor, still plagued with technical problems, was not really ready for market after all. He felt his only option was to proceed with further technical work in order to improve his product.

DISCUSSION POINTS

1. How will you prepare and issue your press releases?

2. How will you ensure that as many of your potential customers as possible know about the release of your new software, while at the same time minimising your costs?

3. If you were to write a review of your own software package for a magazine read by your typical customer, how would you ensure it has the best possible chance of being published and what would it say?

7
Selling Your Software

However brilliantly conceived and written your software is it will never sell itself. It has to be sold; *you* have to sell it. This chapter looks at the process of selling software right from the techniques used to stimulate customer interest in the first place, to making the sale and what happens after the sale is made.

STIMULATING INTEREST

You again need to think of the selling process from the customers' point of view. Before buying your software, customers will:

- Have to know it exists.

- Be attracted by the software and its apparent benefits.

- Probably like to see a demonstration of it.

- Want to be convinced by an 'expert' that the software's apparent benefits are real, and that the software really does have the ability and features to solve their problems.

- Need to be assured that the software is of very high quality and that it is likely to be further developed and supported.

- Want to be convinced that your software package is, among all others, the most suitable for their particular needs.

Software packages only sell if customers know about them. After considering the use of advertisements, mail shots, magazine reviews, etc. as methods of bringing your software to the attention of potential customers, you must concentrate on making the sales themselves, and on planning to ensure that sales can be consistently made over a long period.

Advertising frequently and regularly

Most advertising is temporary. A magazine advert, press release or magazine review is only as permanent as the single issue of the magazine it is displayed in: a month or week. Trade shows typically only last for one or two days. Unless customers are frequently reminded that your software exists they will soon forget about it or, worse, assume that it is no longer being sold.

A policy of continual advertising will counter this threat and provide customers with the assurance that your software is both currently available and being actively promoted and developed.

A good plan is to choose one or two of the most applicable specialist or trade magazines that you originally targeted with your initial advertising, and to place a similarly designed advertisement in each edition, or in every other edition from now on. In this way customers will regularly notice your advertising and will be encouraged to believe that your software is successful, that you support it, and that it will continue to be around for some time.

Magazines and trade journals will probably carry the bulk of your advertising material. However, this should ideally be backed up by at least one other method of advertising and preferably more than one. Trade shows should be attended as frequently as possible and mail shots, if used, should be carried out regularly, say every two to three months.

'Free' advertising methods should be used as much as possible. An on-going series of press releases can be produced and distributed to appropriate magazines covering different aspects of your software's use, pricing and availability. Similarly magazine reviews can form an on-going source of free advertising, whoever they are written by. Initial reviews are likely to concentrate on the software itself, its main features and capabilities. After one review has been published editors may consider publishing further reviews of your software, so long as they are new and sufficiently interesting.

You could even plan a series of reviews, each covering a different aspect of your software and how it might be of use to people. For instance, consider

- writing a review which describes the software's use and benefits to a broad group of people,

- followed by a later review concentrating on how a single person or company has.and continues to benefit from your software,

- followed by another review describing how your software can be used to solve a specific task a large number of customers will have to perform,

- followed by a review illustrating some advanced uses of your software.

And so on. You get the message. A continuing series of adverts, reviews, mail shots and press releases provide an on-going mechanism for bringing your software to the attention of customers and stimulating their interest.

Announcing special offers
Nothing attracts customer interest more than special offers, reduced prices and discounts. If the customer perceives your software to be of benefit in the first place, a reduced price or special deal might be enough to convert this initial interest into an actual sale.

Software companies use various marketing ploys and special offer schemes to tempt customers into buying their products, including:

- special introductory prices

- special lower prices for a limited period

- special lower prices for group or club members and magazine readers

- trade-in schemes for users of competitors' products

- special upgrade prices.

Giving introductory discounts
First, consider offering customers a special introductory discount on your new software package for a limited period. This means, immediately after your software is launched, offering customers a special discount if they buy before a certain date after which you have stated that your software will be available only at its normal full price. Many new software packages are sold in this way. Interested customers will fear that if they do not buy the software quickly they will be forced to pay the full, often much higher price, when the introductory offer ends. This is enough to prompt many customers to buy now rather than later.

Reducing prices temporarily

Temporarily reducing the price of your software can also work to increase sales at any time, long after any initial introductory offer has expired. For this to work you must have been previously seen to be selling your software at a higher price over a reasonably long period of time.

Then for a fixed, limited period you can offer your software to all customers at a special discount, before informing them that the price will again return to its normal level on a certain date. This will again provide many customers with the extra incentive they need to buy your software.

Offering 'exclusive' discounts

You can also use special offer schemes to target specific groups of customers: club members, user groups, existing users, new users, and the readers or subscribers of the magazines in which you advertise. Customers will be attracted by these more 'exclusive' special offers, which should again be made temporarily available to encourage immediate customer response.

Stealing customers from your competitors

Users of competitors' products can often be tempted to switch to your product by inviting them to trade in their existing software in return for yours – at special rates. With trade-in schemes like this customers are only asked to prove ownership of a competitor's product, rather than to relinquish it altogether, before becoming entitled to your software at its discounted price.

Disgruntled users of competitors' software are certain to be interested in switching to another product, and a trade-in scheme might provide them with an inexpensive method of doing so.

Rewarding existing customers

Further versions (upgrades) of your software package can be offered to existing customers at specially reduced prices. Most of your existing customers will be interested in buying your improved software, and all will expect to be rewarded for their loyalty to your product. You can ensure their continued custom and reward their loyalty by offering them your upgraded software on special terms, typically at around fifty per cent of the normal retail price. (The process of upgrading software is fully discussed in chapter 9.)

SELLING THE BENEFITS

Customers are selfish. Once stimulated and attracted to your software, they will want to know what it can do for them. In other words customers want to know how they alone will *benefit* by buying your software. Simply listing the features of your software will lead to few sales. You can ensure that maximum sales are made by persuading customers that your software can

- solve their real-life problems

- save them money or time

- empower them

- entertain them

- give them an edge over their friends or rivals.

Benefits rather than features sell software. Furthermore, if customers perceive that the person describing the benefits of the software is also an 'expert' they are much more likely to be convinced into parting with their money. This is great news for you because, as the developer of the software, you are already an expert in your field and therefore an ideal salesperson for it.

Demonstrating your software

Other than by advertising, there are various ways a small software company can sell the benefits of its software:

- Product demonstrations

- Face-to-face selling

- Telephone contact.

The best way of convincing customers of the benefits of your software is by demonstrating it to them directly. For smaller, cost-conscious software companies and individuals this can be achieved by

- producing freely available demonstration software

- or by arranging software demonstrations at
  - trade shows or exhibitions
  - customers' premises
  - your own premises.

The most cost-effective way of demonstrating the benefits of your software is to produce a demonstration version of the software, and make it freely available for all customers to try out on their own computers and in their own time. Successful demonstration software

- is normally distributed free (or at a nominal charge refundable when the full version is purchased)

- shows off all the main benefits, features and attractions of the full version

- is a pleasure to use in its own right

- is closely representative of the full version

- advertises the full version in some way

- is missing some key feature(s) which renders the software impractical for use other than for demonstration purposes.

Customers are encouraged to use the demonstration version as much as possible in order to discover its benefits for themselves. They are often also actively encouraged to copy the demonstration software and to pass it on to others who may themselves try it and pass it on. In this way as many customers as possible are able to trial your software at minimal cost to you.

Having impressed your customers with the demonstration version they will now have the information they require to order your full version. So displayed somewhere within the demonstration software should be details of your business name, address and telephone number. Pricing and other details of the full version may also be included.

Demonstrating your software at trade shows

Trade shows provide an excellent way of demonstrating the benefits of your software to a large number of appropriate customers, in the same place over a short period. This method is cost-effective too. As an expert you will be able to show many more potential customers the benefits of your software than you ever could by arranging individual demonstrations at customer sites or your own premises.

Visiting customers

Many customers expect software suppliers to come to their premises. This is particularly true with business customers who are looking to buy more expensive software. Though visits to a customer's premises might involve travel, and possibly overnight stays, the costs of this can often be outweighed by the increased probability of making a sale. After your visit and possibly a 'free lunch', the customer will feel more bound to buy your software. Customer visits also have other advantages.

- You are able to discuss the customer's needs face-to-face and in much more detail.

- The customer will probably have more time to view your software.

- Your demonstration can be specificically geared to the needs of the individual customer.

- Even if the customer does not buy your software straight away, he/she will at least be aware of its capabilities and future business is still a possibility.

Inviting customers to your own premises

Using your own premises for demonstration purposes might be appropriate so long as

- your premises are respectable and large enough

- customers are locally based and do not have to travel far.

Remember too that you may need to provide such things as extra chairs, office furniture, refreshments and extra staff to cover the day-to-day duties that cannot be performed while you are entertaining potential customers.

Did you know?

1. Most users (over four in every five) do not make back up or security copies of even their most important software or data.

2. Computer trade shows are popular. Over ten per cent of all computer users have attended at least one.

3. The Internet has around 40 million users worldwide. This figure is growing rapidly.

MAKING THE SALE

Once the customer has been shown the benefits of your software the next stage is to secure the sale itself.

Securing mail order sales

For products that are sold largely by mail order, mail shots and targeted advertising, whether or not customer interest is successfully converted into a real sale often depends on simple mechanics. Once the customer has made up his or her mind to buy your software, you must make it extremely easy to order or buy it. You can do this by

- ensuring the customer knows exactly what is available and at what price

- ensuring the customer knows where and who to contact to buy/ order the software

- providing an easy way for the customer to pay for it

- offering swift delivery times

- offering some form of support, help or advice service after the sale is made.

Make yourself easily contactable by giving your own or your company name, your full address including post code, your telephone and fax numbers including standard dialling codes and, if applicable, the international dialling code that foreign customers may need to use when contacting you by telephone.

It may also be appropriate to state when you can be contacted, for example between 9am and 5pm on weekdays. If you do not mention your hours of business you risk customers calling, only to be disappointed when they discover you are not there. They may be tempted to order a competitor's product instead.

Provide the customer with alternative, easy methods of payment including at least

- all major credit cards

- personal and company cheques

- postal orders and international money orders.

Once customers have made up their minds to order your software they will tend to want to have use of it as soon as possible. Therefore as an extra incentive you should consider offering a rapid, possibly overnight or insured delivery service.

To remove any possible final barriers to the sale, state clearly your policy with regard to the extent of any after-sales help and support you are prepared to offer. This might be minimal for software such as games, but for complex business packages, upon which customers are likely to rely heavily after the initial purchase, the question of support, help and advice is important. So consider offering free support and advice for an initial, limited period: say thirty, sixty or ninety days, backed up with a full no-quibble, money-back guarantee if the customer finds the software is not what was required up to, say, fourteen days after the purchase. Make it clear that any such guarantees are over and above the customer's statutory rights.

Selling face-to-face
Selling by mail order is much less daunting than selling directly to a customer who is standing in front of you, and for most small software companies much more common. Nevertheless, face-to-face selling ability is a prerequisite when attending trade shows or product demonstrations at your own or customers' premises.

The buyer in a face-to-face selling situation will become interested in the product through looking at it or examining it. The salesman's job is to home in on the buyer to turn this interest into a sale.

Being positive and removing obstacles
As a face-to-face salesperson you should appear confident and relaxed when selling your product. Answer all customer questions and concerns in a positive way and maintain an up-beat style.

A normal trend is for buyers to raise obstacles to making the purchase. In fact they are challenging the salesperson to persuade

The best software sales people are

Patient
Accurate
Punctual
Polite
Positive
Confident
Persuasive
Smartly dressed
Knowledgeable
Understanding
Good listeners
Persistent
Helpful
Cheerful

Fig. 7. The qualities of a successful software salesperson.

them that these obstacles can easily be overcome, or that really they do not exist at all. As each obstacle is removed the buyer becomes increasingly confident that the intended purchase will be a good one.

Closing the sale

Unless the buyer has already directly expressed a willingness to buy the software, at the appropriate moment the seller should attempt to secure the sale by presenting the buyer with a stark choice. Something like 'Shall I wrap the software up for you?', or 'Are you intending to pay by cheque?' will force an answer one way or the other from the buyer. If all barriers and obstacles have been removed, and the customer perceives the purchase represents value for money and will deliver the promised benefits, then the sale will be made. If it is not, then some barriers still exist in the customer's mind. Determine them and proceed to remove them.

OFFERING THE CUSTOMER MORE

When a sale is made, especially your first software sale, it is a time to rejoice. To have earned money from the software you have designed and written, toiled over and documented, is an extremely rewarding and gratifying experience. So much so that you may feel like allowing the customer to leave your trade show stand or put the phone down without any further sales effort on your part.

Resist the temptation. Do not start to celebrate yet. There is more selling work to do. How about offering the customer more? Depending on the nature of your software package you could offer the customer:

- An extended telephone support service, whereby for an annual fee customers with problems or questions can make an unlimited number of telephone calls to you for help and advice.

- A software installation and configuration service.

- Training.

- Consultancy, to help the customer take full advantage of the software.

- The professional version when the customer has only bought the standard version.

- Discounts on further copies of your software.

- Extra copies of the documentation.

- Extra complimentary software which enhances or works alongside your main software package.

The customer can only say no. If this does happen you will still have made a sale. If the customer says yes then more income will have been generated, often with a lot less effort than was required to make the initial sale.

CASE STUDIES

Dave becomes a salesman for the first time

Dave's technically superb game started selling well. Two complimentary reviews in different specialist games magazines resulted in twenty-five hard sales and a further 245 requests for his demonstration version. The monthly computer magazine carrying his demonstration version on its cover disk reached over 100,000 readers and resulted in a further 225 sales of his full version.

Spurred by this initial success, Dave continued to regularly advertise his game in two games publications, and sent further copies of his demonstration version to other computer magazines in the hope that they too would distribute it on their cover disks. As Dave had predicted, sales from customers using shareware vendors and bulletin boards were slow to begin with, but did pick up later as this slightly slower distribution method began to take effect.

Dave also demonstrated his software personally at several computer clubs. This resulted in an average of three sales at each venue and allowed Dave to distribute a further seventy-five copies of his demonstration version to interested club members.

Although pleasantly surprised with initial sales Dave noticed that interest in his game seemed disproportionately high. He sensibly concluded that more sales effort would be required to convert this interest into hard sales.

Janette finds most of her customers want telephone support

All Janette's potential customers were understandably cautious at the prospect of using new software to calculate employees' salaries. What if something should go wrong? Janette quickly realised that more customers would buy her software if she was to offer a comprehensive telephone support service backed up by training courses and consultancy services when required. She resolved to provide an initial period of thirty days' free telephone support after which customers could, if required, pay an annual fee for unlimited further access to telephone help and advice. She quickly mailed her 300 initial contacts with her revised list of services and this immediately resulted in a further thirty sales.

Face-to-face selling was Janette's forte. Although regular mail shots were her primary method of advertising Janette found it easy to demonstrate the benefits of her software directly to customers, at both trade shows and visits to customers' premises, and many sales were made as a result.

Lance makes his first sale

Despite the number of other word processors in the market, and Lance's first faltering attempts at marketing, he was finally able to make his first sale – to an old friend. Lance's friend found the software quite impressive but still a little 'buggy' and missing some features he regarded as standard in other word processors. However, he saw potential and offered Lance a partnership deal. He would market and sell the software whilst Lance fixed these outstanding bugs and prepared another, more reliable, version. Lance reluctantly agreed. Lance's friend, already in sales, immediately went to work, preparing numerous reviews, press releases and advertisements.

Lance soon began to realise that sales and marketing skills were just as important as technical skills, if not more so.

DISCUSSION POINTS

1. Where and how frequently will you advertise your software?

2. How will you ensure that customer interest in your software is converted into real sales?

3. What other products or services could you offer to your customers at the time a sale is made?

8
Winning and Keeping Customers

Customers are your life blood. You should devote your best efforts to ensuring that you

- attract as many new customers as possible

- hold on to existing customers.

ATTRACTING NEW CUSTOMERS

How does a small software business attract new customers?

A continuing series of press releases and advertisements will help, as will frequent mail shots, magazine reviews, trade show visits and special offers, but other methods could be used to attract new customers:

- recommendations and referrals

- bundling deals

- time-limited 'free' fully working software

- other markets.

Encouraging customers to recommend your software

Reputations spread quickly by word of mouth, and new customers will often buy software based on a personal recommendation from a friend or colleague already using the software. Your existing customers can be offered incentives like free upgrades, special discounts on further purchases or cash back schemes for any recommendations they make leading to new sales.

Referrals are firmer recommendations – in some cases almost instructions to use a particular piece of software. For example, franchise owners typically distribute a start-up pack to new franchisees. This pack often contains software to get the new franchise up and running. Most new franchisees would happily accept what amounts to a firm recommendation from the franchise owner to use this software and would not even consider using alternative software. So if the franchise owner, or any other type of customer likely to be in a position to make a referral, can be persuaded to adopt your software as standard, more sales to new customers will be made.

Bundling your software with another product

Bundling is where two or more complementary software packages (usually from different software companies) are offered together at a single, usually discounted price. Bundling is sometimes used to introduce new products alongside older, established products or when software companies need to clear old stock prior to releasing a new version. For software suppliers, the large number of new customers acquiring their product offsets the smaller profit made on each copy sold. Software games are often sold this way.

Offering 'free' time-limited software

A popular method of attracting new customers is to give your fully working software to them at no charge at all – at least not right away. The idea is to advertise that your software is available free of charge for say an initial thirty-day period, after which if the customer likes it the product can be bought at the normal price. If the customer decides not to buy your software he simply returns it to you with no further obligation.

You can be reasonably confident that once your software is installed and in use on the customer's computer, there is every likelihood that a full sale will be made when the customer notices that your software, which they have come to rely on, has suddenly stopped working.

This method of attracting new customers is particularly suited to business software.

Exploring other markets

Another way to encourage new business and win new customers is to consider your software's applicability to other related markets. For example, if your software handles the appointments system at doctors' surgeries then, with little or no modification, it could be made appropriate to dental surgeries, chiropractors, opticians and

CUSTOMER RECORD

Name   Any Trading Co.   **Contact**   A. Person

Address   1   12, Some Street

         2   Some Ind. Estate

         3   Some District

Town   4   Bristol

Count(r)y   5   Avon

Post code   BS00 2XX   **Telephone** (0117) 123456

                                Fax   (0117) 123457

Customer type   Retailer   (Head Office)

Purchases

Date	Item	Version	Cost	Resulted from
12/11/95	Bus.Pay.Gold	1.00	199.99	Mailshot
13/12/95	Bus.Pay.Gold	2.00	99.99	Phoning cust.
16/12/96	Telephone support	–	90.00	Info pack

Sales Leads

Date	Query/Interest	Follow up	Resulted from
15/12/96	Telephone support	Faxed info pack	Call from cust.
31/01/97	Training courses	Mailed training info	Trade show

Next contact due   28/2/97

Fig. 8. A typical entry on the customer database.

any other business which works largely on an appointments basis. Similarly, if your software is used to plan training schedules for runners, then consider its suitability to other kinds of athletes like cyclists or swimmers.

BUILDING A CUSTOMER DATABASE

To ensure that you make the maximum possible sales, it is necessary to record details of the customers and potential customers who have bought or expressed an interest in buying your product. By knowing who and where your customers or potential customers are you will be able to contact them to

- follow up their initial interest

- offer them further products or services.

The best way of recording customer details is to set up a **customer database** – a collection of names, addresses and other relevant information which will enable you to quickly discover:

- what products or services customers have purchased

- when purchases were made

- the date you last spoke with or contacted the customer

- a list of products or services your customer has expressed an interest in

- the types of customer buying and expressing interest in your software.

In its simplest form your customer database might consist of a small collection of postcard-sized sheets of paper filed together in alphabetical order; this will be quite adequate for part-time software authors. For those intending to earn a full-time living from writing and selling software, a computerised customer database offering advanced database searching facilities would be more appropriate.

The next problem to solve is what information to keep on your customers. This will be entirely dictated by what you hope to use your database for. Figure 8 shows a typical customer database entry that might be applicable to both part- and full-time software authors.

The Data Protection Act

A word of caution. The Data Protection Act of 1986 requires all companies, businesses, and most government and public offices which hold individuals' personal details in some kind of information retrieval system, to register with the **Data Protection Registrar**. If you intend to hold personal data on your customers (this includes names, addresses, telephone numbers, etc.) *for business purposes*, you should investigate whether you need to register under the Act. The address of the Data Protection Registrar is

Data Protection Registrar
Springfield House
Water Lane
Wilmslow
Cheshire
SK9 5AF Tel: (01625) 535711.

FOLLOWING UP NEW SALES LEADS

A sales lead is simply an opportunity to sell your product to an interested customer. Interested customers will contact you to

- request further details of your software

- request a demonstration version of your software

- ask specific questions.

Your task as a salesman is to

- record their interest on the customer database

- answer their query or request

- convert this interest into a sale.

Gathering customer details

Every time an interested customer calls you have an opportunity to sell your software either right away or in the future. However, first you must know *who* you are speaking with, *why* they have called and *how* you can be of help to them. This means establishing at a minimum:

- the customer's name

- a contact address

- the reason the customer called (the customer's areas of interest).

Before dealing with the specific request for help, ask for the customer's name and contact address. In return promise to send your latest brochure or product information sheet, and possibly a demonstration copy of your software so that the customer can try it out. Record these details as soon as you are given them.

Next, establish and note down the customer's particular concerns or areas of interest.

Giving useful, positive help

Most customers contacting you for information or advice are actually close to buying your software. Perhaps they have established a short-list of two or three products from which their final choice will be made. You can help them select *your* software by answering all of their queries helpfully, confidently and positively. Try to identify and remove any barriers to the sale and particularly emphasise the following.

- How your software solves the customer's problem.

- The new capabilities the customer will have if he or she buys your software.

- The extra time and money the customer will save by using your software.

- The quality, ease of use and permanence of your software.

- How the customer can take delivery of the software the very next day if required.

Even if a sale is not made immediately, you will still have recorded the customer's name, contact details and the nature of their query. All this information can be stored in your customer database for later use.

KEEPING EXISTING CUSTOMERS

New customers are always welcome. Existing customers, on the other hand, cost less to sell to and are often a small software company's main source of sales revenue and profit. This is because existing customers

- are easy to find

- do not require costly demos – they already own your software

- are already convinced of the benefits of your software and are therefore much easier to sell to

- tend to buy further software and services after their initial purchase

- may be reliant on your software and therefore unable to switch to a competitor's product even if they wanted to.

Retaining loyalty

It is easy to see why existing customers are so valuable, but how can you ensure that your customers remain loyal after their initial purchases? You can do this by:

- continuing to provide a quality service

- establishing customer's trust and respect

- ensuring all customer requests and queries are dealt with promptly and professionally

- regularly contacting customers to discuss their needs and problems

- establishing a group of users (a 'user group') to which the customer can belong and benefit from.

Providing quality service
- Be easily contactable by telephone, letter or in person to provide quality help and advice as promptly as possible.

- Be polite, efficient and business-like at all times.

- Talk to customers as one professional does to another.

- Take an active interest in customers' problems.

- Deliver your product or services on time and to a high standard.

- Keep promises.

- Charge a reasonable price for your products and services.

Quality service means lots of other things too (dealt with in more detail in chapter 11). To judge the kind of service you need to provide in order to win and keep existing customers, ask yourself what kind of service *you* would wish to receive from the supplier of a software package that you have bought. This is the kind of service your customers will expect from you.

Staying in contact with your customers
Staying in contact with existing customers is essential if you are to keep them. Contact can be achieved in many ways: through mail shots, mailed newsletters and information sheets, through upgrade offers and offers of other services through telephoning or even visiting customers occasionally to ask if all is well.

Above all, software customers like to be kept informed of:

- new products and new versions of your software

- solutions you have provided to known software problems

- price changes and special offers

- any new service you offer

- your future plans to remain in the market.

You can ensure this kind of information reaches your customers by incorporating it into your press releases, advertisements and mail shots. You might even consider preparing and distributing a regular newsletter as a method of keeping your customers informed.

Producing newsletters
Newsletters can be produced cheaply and easily by anyone who

has access to a computer and a printer – that is, most software authors. Newsletters can contain far more information than advertisements or magazine reviews ever could, and will enhance your image of permanence and professionalism if prepared and presented in the right way.

Successful newsletters usually contain

mostly factual information

news of recent software developments

news of special offers

solutions to known software 'bugs'

a handy hints and tips section

news of forthcoming events

possibly a little advertising material

One or two longer articles in the newsletter may also illustrate how individual, named customers use and benefit from certain features of the software.

The principal aim of a newsletter is to inform rather than to advertise, and to encourage customers to believe that they are vital members of an overall group having a major role to play in the future developments of the software. Your newsletters should be prepared accordingly.

Existing customers will often contact you

When customers contact you, requesting advice, do your utmost to provide them with the information they need immediately. If this is not possible, promise to get back to them as soon as you have found the information they require.

If written information is requested, this should be forwarded on quality stationery, by first class mail. Consider telephoning the next day to ensure that your customer both received and understood your reply.

Did you know?

1. There are more than fifty general computer magazines on sale in the UK.

2. Software purchased from a retail outlet can be up to twice as expensive as that charged by a software mail order company.

3. Most of the copy protection mechanisms used to protect software can easily be circumvented by experienced computer programmers.

USING THE CUSTOMER DATABASE

Your customer database is your prime source of information on potential and existing customers. The sole purpose of holding such information is to enable you to *maximise your sales*. It is therefore essential that all customer information held is both accurate and up-to-date.

Your database will then enable you to:

• follow up initial customer interest

• remain in contact with, and sell to, existing customers

• monitor interest levels and sales success rates

• monitor customer buying patterns

• collect feedback from customers.

Converting customer interest into sales

First, your database can be used to gather a list of the names and addresses of all potential customers whose recorded initial interest has yet to be converted into a sale. These are the customers most likely to respond to your further or follow-up advertising material – usually mail shots containing full product information or special offer details – backed up with 'easy to order – easy to pay' facilities.

Ensure any sales resulting from your follow-up contacts are also noted and that your customer database is updated accordingly.

Selling to existing customers

A list of existing customers can also be retrieved from your database. Existing customers may have already registered their interest in new or enhanced products, and new services and all such interest will have been recorded.

Follow-up contacts can again be made to secure further sales.

Depending on the nature of your database, much more refined searches can also be made to highlight groups of customers. For instance you might require a list of all customers

- currently owning the 'standard' version of your software

- and who have also expressed an interest in upgrading to your professional version within the last six months.

These customers could then be targeted with advertising material specifically emphasising the extra benefits available from using the professional version.

Monitoring buying patterns and sales success rates

Your customer database can also be used to determine and establish the buying patterns of your customers so that you might

- identify and rectify any weaknesses in your advertising and selling methods

- exploit new selling opportunities.

For instance, you may be interested in knowing how many customers bought your product within six months of registering their initial interest. If this figure is low then you will have immediately identified an area where a larger number of potential sales could be made. Similarly your database could be used to establish:

- The effectiveness of your various advertising campaigns (by recording what influenced the customer to buy or request further information about your product).

- How many customers bought your 'lite', standard and professional versions.

- How many customers bought your software after first trying your demonstration version.

- How many customers bought software during special offer periods and how many bought at the full price.

Collecting feedback and customer requests

Your customer database can also be used to collect information such as the level of customer satisfaction with your software, and customer requests for new features and capabilities. It can also be used to collect details of requests for new products, and for new or improved services.

All this information can be retrieved from your database, collated and examined. This will help you provide:

(a) quality software continually developed in line with customer requirements

(b) the quality service your customers have asked for

(c) new products or services that many of your customers will purchase.

CASE STUDIES

Dave actively seeks new customers

Dave had always realised that most of his sales would come from new customers, since existing users of his game would rarely buy further copies. Nevertheless, he felt it worthwhile to initiate a paper-based customer records system, just in case.

To increase sales to new customers, Dave sought a partner for a games bundling deal. This policy worked well and although Dave's profit per copy sold was reduced, the higher level of sales resulted in a higher than expected overall profit. Dave had also invited customer feedback on his game and, from his customer database, noted that a large number of customers had expressed a strong desire for an enhanced, more challenging version of his game – enough to convince Dave that development of such a version should begin straight away.

Janette creates a sophisticated customer database

Aware that most of her sales would come from existing users, requiring product enhancements in line with annual changes to tax and NI regulations, Janette resolved to build a sophisticated customer database to carefully monitor her customers and keep them informed of the latest developments.

To win new customers Janette decided to offer free 'time limited' versions of her software to all customers requesting it. She incorporated this new offer into both her latest mail shots and her bi-monthly newsletter. After a further three months, sales of her payroll software were well up. Also up was the sales revenue generated from new telephone support agreements and training courses.

Conscious of the approaching autumn budget, and spurred by customer requests for additional software features, Janette decided that now was the time to start looking for permanent programming staff.

Lance appears to be on the right road at last

Although Lance continued to work on solving known problems and implementing new features into his word processor, he was delighted to find that sales of his initial release began to materialise. He secretly knew that this was largely attributable to the fine sales work of his new partner, who managed to persuade customers to buy Lance's current release with the guarantee that the next version of the software would be supplied free of charge.

Lance also set up a computerised customer database to carefully record all new sales. When his enhanced software was ready all existing customers were listed from the database and sent free copies – as promised.

Meanwhile sales of the new version also began to pick up as a direct result of the new, effective advertising and sales policies of Lance's partner.

DISCUSSION POINTS

1. Where will most of your sales revenue come from – new or existing customers – and why?

2. How will you keep track of your customers?

3. What measures will you take to ensure that your customers are kept fully informed of the latest developments in your software?

9
Upgrading Your Software

Upgrading software simply means improving it in some way: making it better, faster or easier to use. No matter how good a software package is it can always be improved. Software authors continually seek ways of improving their software and take great pride in demonstrating the advances they have made. However, the real reasons commercial software is upgraded are

- to make extra sales

- to satisfy customer and legal requirements

- to remain competitive.

WHY UPGRADE?

Making money from upgrading your software

The primary motive for producing an improved version of your software is to make further sales. The logic is that whatever your current level of sales, given the same selling expertise and pricing policy, more copies of your software will be sold if it is a better product.

Customers require software upgrades

Another reason to upgrade your software is that your customers have asked you to or *require* you to do so. Customers who have asked for improvements are generally also willing to pay a reasonable price for them.

Upgrading software to remain competitive

The software market is in a continual state of rapid change – existing software continues to be improved upon and new software packages appear daily. There is a real possibility that if your software is not upgraded in line with new market trends, new legal regulations and the products of your competitors, your customers will quickly lose interest in your software, preferring a more up-to-date and usable product.

DO YOU NEED TO UPGRADE?

The following checklists detail some of the common reasons software is upgraded, and will help you determine whether, and approximately how often, to upgrade.

Do you need to upgrade your software?

1. Does your software require changing if, for example, legal, taxation or statutory regulations change? (Janette's payroll package certainly does, Dave's game probably does not). *Yes/No*

2   Have customers reported any problems or bugs with your software? *Yes/No*

3. Have any customers expressed a desire for you to improve your software in some way? *Yes/No*

4. Would you find an improved version of your software easer to sell to your customers? *Yes/No*

5. Do you feel that you must upgrade software to remain competitive in the software market? *Yes/No*

6. Do you need to modify your software so that it can be used on other types of computers? *Yes/No*

7. By upgrading your software, could it be made usable by a larger number of potential customers? *Yes/No*

If you have answered Yes to *any* of the above, it is likely that you will need to upgrade your software at least once. If you have answered Yes to questions 1 or 5 then consider upgrading your software on a regular basis.

How often do you need to upgrade?

1. Does your current software release suffer from major bugs or a larger number of smaller bugs causing customer discontent? *Yes/No*

If *Yes* consider preparing an upgraded version of your software which fixes all known bugs immediately.

2. Is your software dependent on current legal or
    other government regulations?   *Yes/No*

    If *Yes* at a minimum an upgrade is required each
    time new regulations come into effect.

3. Is your software simple and easy to learn?   *Yes/No*

    If *Yes* consider upgrading it every six to twelve
    months subject to 1 and 2 above.

4. Is your software complex, requiring much effort to
    learn and lots of experience to use efficiently?   *Yes/No*

    If *Yes* then, subject to 1 and 2 above, consider
    producing upgrades every eighteen to twenty-four
    months.

If you have answered *No* to all of the above then consider upgrading your software every nine to eighteen months.

LISTENING TO CUSTOMERS

Producing software upgrades involves writing new, or modifying existing, software. Unless your upgrade is very minor it will be necessary to draw up a new project plan for what *will* be in effect a new product.

Just as with your initial software release, your first step should always be to find out what improvements and enhancements *customers* want you to make to your software. This means listening to their comments and requests, noting them down and building a new customer requirements list. As before this list should be formally drawn up, rationalised and ordered in a logical way.

After analysing the new requirements lists, the next stage is to form an upgrade project plan with estimates for each phase of the new project (design, software development, testing, documentation, launch).

Modifying existing marketing plans

Depending on the extent of your improvements and changes, estimates for each phase will probably be lower than for your original release. Much of the original design documentation, software and manuals will require amending, rather than writing

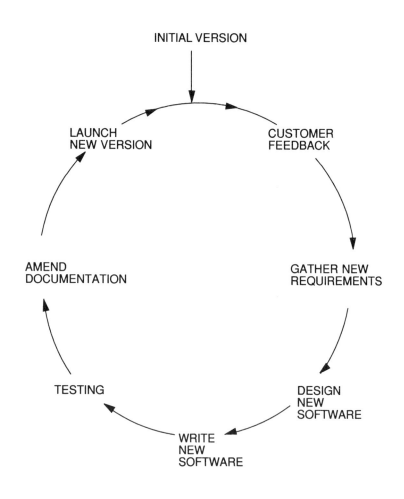

Fig. 9. The software upgrade cycle.

from scratch again.

Similarly, marketing plans might need to be modified to cater for the forthcoming release of a new version of your software.

Certainly a new series of press release, adverts and mail shots will need to be planned and prepared. This time your aims are to inform as many customers and potential customers as possible that

- your software already exists

- it is already successful

- a new, improved version of it is about to be released.

Upgrade work moves in cycles, as shown in Figure 9. Customer requests for improvements lead to further design work, further software development, more testing, modified documentation and finally to a new version release. Once the new version has been released, customers begin to request further changes and so the cycle goes round again.

Increasing your software version number

Each time round the cycle the software version number is increased. For major upgrades increase the full version number (version 1.00 becomes 2.00), for less substantial upgrades increase the version number by 0.1 (1.00 becomes 1.10) and for a very minor upgrade increase the version number by 0.01 (1.00 becomes 1.01).

Pricing your upgraded software

Depending on your individual circumstances, consider offering your upgraded software at the same price as your previous version to all new customers. For existing customers it is common to offer a discounted price to encourage them to buy your latest version. Existing customers typically expect to pay around half the normal price that new customers pay for the upgraded version. If appropriate you might also continue to sell your older version at a reduced price.

Occasionally, special upgrade agreements made with customers mean that, for say an annual charge, all upgrades during the year are distributed free. For example, a new customer buying Janette's payroll software for £200 might pay an extra £130 per year to effectively pay in advance for any further releases of the software during the next year. This fee is paid regardless of whether any upgrades are actually issued during the year.

IMPROVING FEATURES AND PERFORMANCE

Software can be upgraded in many ways but most upgrade work involves satisfying customer demands for

- new software features (the ability of the software to handle new tasks, or to handle existing tasks more efficiently)

- increased performance (increased program running speed)

- solutions ('fixes') to known software problems.

Adding new features

New software features are almost always welcome by both customers and software authors. New features provide customers with the ability to carry out all sorts of new tasks, as well as making their existing tasks much easier. For software authors, new features are welcome because they make software:

- easier to sell

- easier to use and more efficient (most of the time)

- more interesting or enjoyable to use

- applicable to a larger number of potential customers.

Your customers will normally dictate what new features are incorporated into your software, though this does not preclude you from including some of your own. Below are some of the new features the case study characters have included in their new software.

Dave's Adventures in Jungleland game

Better game music, the animals and background drawn more realistically, new game animals, new methods of points scoring, new animal sounds, faster game play, new weapons to fight with, new landscapes to cross, new methods of defence and the new ability to use a joystick.

Janette's Business Payroll Gold

Amended methods of calculating tax and NI in line with new

regulations, improved speed of operation, several new management reports, enhanced on-line help, new ability to handle employees paid every four calendar weeks and a more efficient method of registering new employees.

Lance's Buzz Word word processor
All known bugs fixed, new ability to check document spelling, ability to write newspaper-style multiple columns, new ability to support to the use of a mouse, ability to enlarge to decrease the size of individual letters, new facility to incorporate pictures into documents.

Beware – new features can also cause problems
New features are generally welcome, but take care not to include too many in your software. As new features are added

- the amount of time required to learn how to use the software may increase

- the software may on occasion become more difficult to use

- the software will tend to run more slowly.

Increasing performance
Increased performance is almost always welcome. In software terms 'slow' means 'inefficient'. Customers having to wait ten minutes for a report to be printed out on the printer will be delighted if an upgraded version of the software cuts this down to two minutes.

Program speed is even more important to some types of software. Games software particularly can be totally unplayable if the software is unable to keep up.

Did you know?
1. A single floppy disk is easily capable of containing the complete works of Shakespeare.

2. The top chess playing program can regularly beat ninety-nine per cent of all chess players.

3. The speed and power of computers is approximately doubling every year at the same price point.

CORRECTING KNOWN PROBLEMS

Software errors or bugs can seriously damage the reputation (and sales) of your software. Major bugs can render a software package unusable by customers. Minor bugs at the very least annoy customers and make their lives more difficult. Even if you have no other reason to upgrade your software, you should still seriously consider doing so if bugs have been found in your existing version.

CUSTOMISING YOUR SOFTWARE

Another way to upgrade software is to customise it for the benefit of individual customers. Typically your software package, like Janette's payroll package, will be designed and written so that as many different customers as possible are able to use it.

Sometimes, however, individual companies may request specific software features they alone might use, and which generally are not applicable to most other customers. For Janette this may take the form of one of her customers requesting extra software to handle, say, a company-specific system of bonus payments. Since this new software is unlikely to be of use to anyone else Janette would be quite able to charge the individual customer a much higher price for producing it.

DEVELOPING A 'SISTER' PRODUCT

If no reason to upgrade your software can be found, then do not upgrade it. It will not be worth your time and effort. Few, if any, new sales will be generated if you do. So where can you go from here?

First continue to advertise and sell the product for as long as customers want it. Next consider whether a new 'sister' product could be developed to work alongside or complement your existing product. For instance, Dave Williams might consider writing a sequel to his adventure game rather than upgrading it. This might result in a new game, Adventures in Desertland, effectively a sister product to, and a likely purchase for all avid players of Dave's first game, Adventures in Jungleland.

A good sister product will:

• Be designed, written and released to the same or better standard than the original.

- Be noticeably similar to the existing product, so that customers are reminded of, or immediately feel at ease with, the new software.

- Be a natural next purchase for customers of the existing software.

- Not rely on the existing software in any way to run.

- Cause customers to regard it as a high quality, usable product in its own right, whether or not they own the existing software.

Developing an entirely new product

If all else fails consider the possibility of developing a completely new software package. This can often be a very sensible and profitable option, even if your existing software continues to sell well. The idea is that as sales of your existing software begin to fall, income is replaced by the increasing sales of your new software. Very often the combined sales of two software packages can be much more lucrative than those made from a single offering.

Remember the basics for developing new software products – ideas, customer requirements, marketing plans, etc. Refer back to chapter 1 for a refresher course if necessary.

Selling older versions of your software

A final note to producing upgrades. However much new versions of software are improved, you may still experience a demand for older versions of your software from customers

- preferring to pay a lower price for older software which they feel is nevertheless still quite adequate for their use

- having older computers not able to run your latest version

- having slow procurement and implementation time scales.

So it is worth at least considering making older versions of your software available for a while. The extra administrative effort involved in selling and supporting two versions of your software, and the possible customer confusion that might result, could well be outweighed by the extra sales revenue received.

CASE STUDIES

Dave provides his customers with an improved game

Prompted by numerous customer requests, Dave started work on an improved, more challenging version of his game. He built a revised list of customer requirements, and again produced and followed new project and marketing plans. The result was strong initial sales of his upgraded version, accompanied by a gradual decline in sales of his existing game.

Dave had considered it worthwhile continuing to sell his original game, and although he experienced some difficulty explaining that two versions of his game were available, many customers at first buying his previous release soon contacted Dave again to buy the improved version at a specially discounted price.

Feeling that further improvements to his game would lead to few extra sales, Dave began work on a sister product, Adventures in Desertland, which when completed sold well to Dave's existing customers and others aware of his fine reputation as a games developer.

Janette updates her software in line with new income tax regulations

Although she had received notification from two customers of small problems associated with her software, and several requests for new product features, Janette realised that the main reason her software must be upgraded was to facilitate forthcoming changes to income tax regulations. Employing a new permanent member of staff to handle software development, Janette set about work designing and documenting her new version. Soon her new version 2.00, priced at the same level as version 1.00 but available to existing customers at half price, was ready.

Sales to new customers continued at around the same level as before. However, overall sales revenue tripled, due mainly to the extra revenue earned from existing customers deciding to upgrade in order to comply with new tax regulations.

Lance's new version leaves customers unsatisfied

Lance's new 'bug free' software was beginning to sell quite well, though not as well as he hoped it would. With his strong technical ability, Lance conceived an idea to provide extra software which used the computer's sound facilities to 'read aloud' documents that had been typed into the computer, and which was also able to enlarge the text on the screen to make it easier to read. Lance's partner agreed that these features would make the software much easier for blind or partially sighted people to use.

This plan appeared to have potential and when the work was completed, sales began well. However, since Lance had never at any stage consulted customers for their requirements, sales soon dropped again as blind and partially sighted customers began to complain that, although well conceived, the new features had been implemented badly and were not all easy to use.

DISCUSSION POINTS

1. Will your software need to be upgraded? If so how often and why?

2. How can your software be upgraded so that the new version has wider applicability to more potential customers?

3. What will you charge both new and existing customers for software upgrades and will you continue to sell your older versions?

10
Maximising Sales and Profits

Profit is what is left after subtracting all costs from all revenue. Any level of profit is welcome but your aim is to *maximise* profits. To do this you need to ensure that

- overall sales revenue is as high as possible

- and overall costs are kept as low as possible.

One is no good without the other. Your aim is to find a level of sales which, given your costs and profit per copy sold, leads to the highest possible overall profit.

Profit versus sales
Total sales revenue is the total received from all sales made. The cost of each copy sold is derived by dividing total costs by the number of copies sold. To maximise overall profits it is clear that total sales revenue needs to be as high as possible and the cost of each copy sold should be as low as possible.

It is important to realise that higher profits cannot be guaranteed simply by setting a higher price. As already seen, as prices rise, demand falls. You must set a price which, given cost per copy, leads to highest profits.

For instance, if each copy of your software package cost £20 to produce but was sold for £30, if you sold 100 copies your profit would be £1,000. However, if you lowered the price to £25 and this resulted in sales of 300 copies then although your profit per copy is lower (£5 as opposed to £10) your overall profit has increased from £1,000 to £1,500 on sales revenue rising from £3,000 to £7,500.

The overall profit figure, as opposed to profit per copy sold, is the important one. In this case, it has been increased simply by reducing the price.

Sometimes profits can also be increased by *raising* price levels.

For instance, if the price was increased to £40 per copy and overall sales reduced from 100 to 75, overall profit would also increase from £1,000 to £1,500.

WHERE ARE YOUR SALES COMING FROM?

To maximise profits you need to know from where your sales revenues are being received (and not received) and what costs are being incurred. Costs and revenue can both be derived from your books of accounts (discussed fully in chapter 11).

In the first instance, sales revenue can be determined from your customer database. For each customer you will have noted the date of sale as well as the price paid. A global search of your database will quickly reveal how many customers bought your software at each of the different prices you charged. Maybe more profit was earned overall on software sold at a lower price during special offer periods, for example. Maybe, by increasing the price, sales fell only slightly and the higher profit on each copy sold contributed to a higher overall profit.

Sources of income

You can also use your customer database to examine the kind of customers buying your software. You are particularly interested to know whether the average backgrounds and characteristics of these customers closely match those of your typical customer. Is your software actually selling to the kind of customers you had originally developed the product for? If not, then why not, and what further steps can be taken to ensure that your typical customer is better served?

You are also interested in finding other groups of customers to whom the software is not selling particularly well.

For instance, by searching her customer database Janette found that for some reason her payroll software was not selling well to companies in the building or manufacturing sectors. After some research she found that these businesses tended not to attend the trade shows she did, so most of them were unaware of the existence of Janette's software. By selecting and subsequently attending a trade show primarily suited to these types of businesses, Janette was soon able to reach and sell to many new customers and as a result her profit increased.

Your customer database can be used to discover all kinds of customer buying trends.

TOTAL SALES REVENUE: £24,000

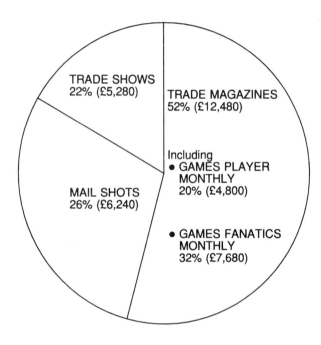

Fig. 10. Sales resulting from different methods of advertising
as gleaned from a typical customer database.

- The type of customers buying and not buying your software.

- Where they live.

- Their age range.

- Their social class.

- The type of business they run.

- The size of their business.

- The frequency of repeat business from each category of customer.

- The number of copies sold at various price levels.

- The effectiveness of advertising in certain publications, mail shots and at trade shows.

- The effectiveness of issuing demonstration copies of your software.

- The number of customers telephoning to buy your software, as opposed to approaching your trade stand or writing to you.

- Your success rate at converting sales leads into actual sales.

The list could go on, but the overall idea is to identify potentially weak areas and find methods of improving your service to, and increasing sales in, these areas. Your customer database becomes an invaluable tool for doing this. The only restriction on the kind of information available from your customer database is the type, extent and accuracy of the information you have recorded on it.

DISCOUNTING AND SPECIAL OFFERS

Customers always like discounts. They feel happier paying a reduced price for the same product. This can also be profitable for you. As previously illustrated reducing the profit per copy can lead to a higher overall profit if proportionately more sales are made.

However, reduced prices and special offers need not only apply to new sales. Software companies use all manner of discounting schemes when selling their software, all with the idea of increasing total profit.

Examples of discounting schemes

- Special introductory prices for new software packages.

- Upgrades at discounted prices to existing customers.

- New software or upgrades at discounted prices for limited periods.

- Older versions at discounted prices.

- Bundling software with other products.

- Free telephone support for limited periods.

- Cheaper, cut down or 'lite' versions for new customers.

- Special prices to certain groups of customers (club members, magazine subscribers, owners of competitors' products, etc.).

- Free upgrades to customers buying within a certain period.

- Discounts for bulk purchases and site licence schemes.

This list is not exhaustive but may give you some ideas for maximising sales and profits of your own software package.

EXPLORING NEW MARKETS

If you feel your current market is as profitable as it can become (an ideal position to be in), do not worry. There are further ideas to explore – all designed to increase your profit even more.

'Generalising' your software

Generalisation is the opposite to customisation. With customisation, software is tailored to the needs of specific individual customers. Generalisation, on the other hand, is the process by which software is modified so that it becomes of use to a wider range of customers. An example of this was making doctors' appointment software applicable to dentists, and making athletes' training schedule software applicable to cyclists and swimmers.

What you need to do now is to consider your own software package and how it might be made applicable to different groups of customers, as well as remaining applicable to existing ones.

Here are some examples of existing products which, with the modifications listed, could be made applicable to new groups of customers.

Existing software	Modification	Possible new markets
Computer games	New 'play and learn' features	Schools, younger children, education markets
Word processor	Foreign language facilities	Foreign customers, language schools
Payroll software	Modified for self-employed people	Any self-employed business or partnership
Library software, monitoring book lending and return	Modifications	Video lending libraries, tool and care hire companies, any type of business lending or hiring items which are returned later
Software monitoring share price movements	Modifications	Currency dealers, commodity dealers
Needlework-designing software	Modifications	Lace designers, knitters, tapestry designers
Horse racing betting software	Modifications	Greyhound racing, any type of sport which involves handicapping and betting.

PROVIDING OTHER SERVICES

Apart from selling software there are plenty of other ways a small software supplier can add to annual profits. These include providing customers with:

- telephone or other forms of product support

- training courses

- consultancy services.

Providing support

Most software companies provide some sort of support service for their customers. This may be as simple as giving a telephone number for customers to use when they find their computers are unable to read the disks the software is contained on. Or it might mean providing chargeable telephone support which customers can use when they experience problems.

In some cases telephone support is provided on the basis that your response to the customer's problem is guaranteed within a certain number of hours. The faster the required response, the more expensive this kind of support will be.

Occasionally customers may even wish to have the option of calling you to their business site in order to resolve a particular problem.

Providing training services

Complex software usually takes time to learn and use efficiently. Some software companies therefore also offer comprehensive training courses to enable their customers to quickly become familiar with their products. Training courses, typically charged for on a 'per student per day' basis, can often be an extremely effective way of increasing overall income and profits.

Offering consultancy services

Consultancy means 'giving advice'. Customers may require your consultancy services in order to determine how best to solve particularly knotty business problems using your software. Consultancy rates can typically range between £200 and £1,000 per day (!) depending on the nature of the consultancy.

Did you know?

1. The top draughts-playing program recently became the world draughts champion.

2. The average street price of a new personal computer is around £600 – £1,000.

3. The average price of a top-selling word processor is around £120.

KEEPING COSTS DOWN

Keeping costs down is important, regardless of the level of sales. By keeping costs to a minimum you will ensure that, given a constant price and level of sales, profits are maximised.

The main costs for smaller software companies and individuals are associated with the time it takes to design and develop software. These costs can be minimised by:

● initially developing software in your spare time

● developing efficient product and marketing plans

● using quality software design and development methods. These will lead to reduced design and development times and a much shorter testing phase.

Other costs, typically incurred later, are those pertaining to advertising, product storage and packaging, attending trade shows, buying equipment, acquiring office premises and employing staff. These can be reduced by various means.

● Careful selection of advertising locations and negotiating special rates for frequently used advertising space.

● Keeping the minimum amount of stock to cater for on-going needs.

● Ensuring that packaging is conveniently shaped (for easy storage) and hard wearing.

● Attending only *relevant* trade shows.

● Purchasing new equipment only when absolutely necessary.

● Initially using your home as your base.

● Employing a minimum number of staff (if any). If you must hire additional personnel, consider hiring part-time rather than full-time staff.

CASE STUDIES

Dave keeps his costs to a minimum

Dave had always kept an eye on costs. Working independently from his own home, he sought special discounted rates from the magazines he regularly used to place his advertisements. The three-day working week he was able to negotiate with his employers also meant that he was able to devote more time to his software business, whilst retaining enough regular income to cover his main household costs.

Using his customer database Dave also examined the number of sales made at various price levels. By reducing his prices slightly he was able to make a proportionately higher number of sales and this in turn resulted in higher overall profits.

Janette profits from training and telephone support

Janette maximised her profits by offering customers a guaranteed eight-hour response system of telephone support backed up with a full training and consultancy service – all of which were readily sought by her customers. In view of this, and in order to encourage more customers to purchase her software, she reduced its price from £199 to £99 and continued to update it regularly in line with government tax regulations. This increased sales markedly, and a number of Janette's new customers went on to spend further money on her support, training and consultancy services.

Janette soon left her full-time job and, despite the cost of renting new office premises and employing new staff, was able to build a very profitable business.

Lance modifies his software to cater for foreign customers

To reach new foreign markets Lance modified his software to enable it to display different languages and character sets. He also procured some special language translation software from another company so that foreign language documents could easily be translated into English and vice versa. Lance also decided that new office space was required to meet his plans for expansion, and a new secretary to handle office administration.

As a result costs rose significantly and, though sales were slightly up, these failed to bring an overall profit. Advertising abroad was also a problem. Further costs were incurred as Lance made expensive international telephone calls to place advertisements in foreign magazines. With little customer requirements for telephone support, training or consultancy, and after making losses for the first two years of trading, Lance began wondering whether all his efforts were worthwhile.

DISCUSSION POINTS

1. How will you ensure that your software is priced at a level designed to bring you maximum profits?

2. Where are your sales coming from and are there any noticeable areas from which sales have been markedly less than expected?

3. What measures can you take immediately which will reduce your costs?

11
Running a Professional Business

You should above all aim to run a professional business. This means adopting a professional, business-like approach to both customers, and internal working methods and procedures. You should be particularly concerned with:

• providing customers with a quality service

• building a solid reputation

• keeping promises

• dealing with people as one professional does with another

• keeping accurate records of accounts.

OFFERING A QUALITY SERVICE

Quality of service, dealt with briefly in chapter 8, is sometimes the only distinguishing factor between rival software companies offering similar products at similar prices. Given a choice most customers will prefer dealing with the company offering prompt, polite and reliable service. You can ensure that you provide quality service by:

• making yourself easily contactable

• making yourself available to talk to customers

• projecting a professional image

• speaking politely and courteously with customers

• using quality, letterheaded paper and stationery when writing to customers

- keeping promises

- being honest and fair

- listening to customers

- being prepared to 'go the extra mile' to help customers with their problems or queries.

Making yourself contactable

You should be easily contactable by post, telephone and preferably fax. Written responses to customer enquiries should be informative, clear, concise and delivered by return of first class post on quality, letterheaded stationery.

Customers telephoning you should expect to hear no more than four telephone rings before the telephone is picked up. If no one is available to take the call then an answering machine should explain this and provide a mechanism for the customer to leave a message.

A fax facility will enable you to promptly send written product and customer information.

Your hours of business should be clearly stated in all advertisements and mail shot material so that customers know when you are contactable.

Presenting a professional image

Equally important is the need to present yourself in a professional business-like way when meeting customers face to face. So dress appropriately. Smart clothes are essential. There is no need to be over-formal but do not dress in jeans or a tee shirt. This will create a bad image and one which you will struggle to shake off.

To customers, your personal image is also the image of your company – and its software. If your personal appearance is smart and professional, customers will naturally assume your company and its products are likewise.

Being polite

Customers always expect to be treated politely and take any signs of impoliteness very personally. If you are perceived as being impolite in any way, there is every possibility that you will not even get the chance to show customers what your software can do – you will have already been shown the door or the telephone will have been hung up.

Remaining courteous and polite in all situations can be difficult.

Customers can sometimes be argumentative or even discourteous to you. However, in line with your professional image, never return any impoliteness. Remain positive, confident and never be drawn into an argument. Customers will often judge your 'real' standard of professionalism by how you act in difficult situations like these and will respect you for continuing to remain calm, unperturbed and cheerful.

KEEPING PROMISES

Customers expect you to deliver on the promises you make. If you assure a customer that the written information they have requested will immediately be sent to them by first class mail, they will expect to receive it the next working day. If it is not received, then the customer may lose interest or buy from someone else. The last thing you want is for customers to contact you a second time with a complaint that you have not done what you had originally promised.

Honesty and fairness

Customers expect to be treated honestly and fairly. If they perceive otherwise, you will quickly lose business as they take their custom elsewhere.

Honesty means admitting mistakes when you are responsible for them – and rectifying them as soon as possible at your own cost. Honesty means explaining to customers the real implications of taking a certain course of action rather than just advising them to take it so as to further increase your sales.

Fairness means refunding customers' money within a realistic period, if the software is found not to be usable for any reason. Fairness also means charging a reasonable fee, and not penal rates, to customers who totally rely on your software in order to run their business.

BUILDING A REPUTATION

If you deliver a quality product, backed up with a professional service, customers will view you and your company in a professional light. They will talk to other customers and before long you will have built yourself a solid reputation.

Reputation is all-important. When faced with the choice of a number of software products, each offering similar facilities, customers are far more likely to choose the one which has been personally recommended to them by a colleague, or which the customer knows is from a company with a solid business reputation.

Conversely companies with bad reputations, earned from poor service or poor quality products, seldom prosper for long. Customers soon learn to avoid dealing with them.

Reputations gradually earned over many months and years can be lost forever overnight. A single piece of bad publicity, if distributed widely enough, can cut sales to zero in a matter of a day or two, never to be regained. So always, always act and deal professionally, honestly and fairly.

Did you know?

1. The response rate to most computer mail shots is under two per cent.

2. Most business software packages come with at least thirty days' free telephone support.

3. Home-users spend more on educational software than they do on any other kind of home software.

KEEPING RECORDS AND ACCOUNTS

All businesses need to keep accurate business records and accounts. Chapter 1 looked at some of the many advantages to be gained from keeping business and accounting records and the customer database as an example of a business record has also been discussed.

Now look at the other types of business records a small software company might keep. These typically include:

- marketing and project plans

- business objectives and deadlines

- customer requirements lists

- design documentation

- program specifications

- testing documentation

INCOME (left-hand page)

Date	Customer	Total Income	Version 1.00	Version 2.00	Telephone support	Training	Other
July	96/97 Running total B/F	5412.98	3732.66	1232.32	323.00	100.00	25.00
1/7	Smiths and Sons	69.99	69.99				
5/7	A. T. Travis	239.99		199.99	40.00		
24/7	Prince Manufacturing	200.00			60.00	140.00	
29/7	Streetwise Trading Co.	99.99	69.99		30.00		
31/7	Global Communications	612.00		500.00	100.00		12.00

EXPENDITURE (right-hand page)

Date	Item	Total expend	Computer equipment	Postage	Telephone	Adverts	Other
July	96/97 Running total B/F	1941.66	1000.00	90.00	53.44	512.00	186.22
1/7	New printer	499.99	499.99				
2/7	Stamps	10.00		10.00			
5/7	Phone bill	52.00			52.00		
9/7	Business Mag. monthly	80.00				80.00	
20/7	Trade show admission	100.00					100.00

Fig. 11. Two facing pages from a cash book.

- magazines, press releases, reviews, etc.

- details of pricing arrangements, special offers and discounting schemes

- original documents relating to the software manuals.

And much more besides.

Business records like these will quickly become indispensable to your business, although you are not actually required to keep them.

However, as a business (large or small) you *are* required by law to keep accounts – financial records of all revenue and expenditure – and to present these, usually annually, to the tax authorities for the purposes of tax assessment.

Recording costs and expenditure

Keeping records of financial transactions worries some people but it need not be frightening. A simple accounts system need only consist of a small book containing a record of all monies paid out (expenditure) and all monies received (income).

It is a good idea to use a book whose pages are divided into two. Use the left-hand side of the page for listing income and the right-hand side for payments, as shown in Figure 11. This will help an accountant reconcile your accounts at the end of the year.

For each item of expenditure simply record the payment date, to whom the money was paid, for what it was paid and the amount. Similarly for income, a date received, from whom received and a description of what the income resulted from.

A simple system like the one shown below in Figure 11 is probably all you will need at first. It is basic, but with it you will be able to:

- see how well the business is doing in financial terms

- reconcile your account with your business bank account statement

- give your accountant all he/she needs when preparing your accounts

- satisfy the requirements of the tax authorities.

Opening a business bank account

You will probably find it useful to open a separate business bank account fairly early on. This will

- make it easy for you to reconcile your accounts

- keep your business and personal finances separate

- be necessary when applying for some kinds of government business development grants.

If you do decide to open a business bank account then shop around before deciding which bank or building society to favour with your custom. Bank charges vary considerably and some banks offer free banking facilities to new businesses for their first twelve months of trading.

Employing an accountant

Depending on the size of your software business you may consider it useful to use an accountant. Accountants can offer all sorts of financial advice to new businesses, and can prepare and submit accounts to the tax authorities in the manner required, on your behalf – leaving you free to do what you do best – developing software. Their advice on taxation and other matters can often save more money in the long run than they charge for their services.

Consider at least contacting one or two local accountants to discuss the services they provide – and their fees. Then make up your own mind. Unless your business is a limited company you are not required by law to use an accountant.

Value Added Tax (VAT)

You are legally obligated to register for VAT if the annual turnover (total value of all the products and services you supply) of your business exceeds £47,000 per year (as from 30th November 1995). For those whose annual turnover is approaching this figure it is possible to apply to register for VAT in advance. For everyone else, registering for VAT will not be applicable.

Registering for VAT is not all bad news. Although you will be required to add a VAT element (currently 17.5%) to the price of your software and pay this back to the Customs and Excise, you will also be able to reclaim the VAT element on all the applicable purchases that you make. So, for example, because VAT is generally chargeable on software sales, you will need to increase the price of your software from, say, £100 to £117.50. However, you will also be able to reclaim £117.50 on the purchase of a computer with a VAT-inclusive price tag of £1,117.50 – a significant saving.

CASE STUDIES

Dave provides his customers with a quality product

Since Dave's games customers required little support, training or consultancy, Dave decided to concentrate on building his reputation through the quality of the games software he supplied. In addition, he made sure that all customer orders were dealt with and dispatched the same working day and always strived to answer his business telephone within four rings. He also purchased an answering machine which he used when he was not able to answer the telephone. Dave responded promptly to all written requests for information and, with his replies, always included a well-presented colour brochure advertising his other products and an attractive compliments slip.

Dave's accounting records were simple, yet accurate and well presented. Each item of expenditure was accompanied by a proper receipt and all incoming funds were detailed in full. Dave presented his accounts annually to the tax authorities who never once queried any of Dave's financial entries.

Janette prospers due to her fine business reputation

Janette's software required updating frequently, due to ever-changing tax and NI regulations, but she always managed to release the new software to all her customers on time and working correctly. Because of this, her perceived professionalism and her willingness to extend the hours of her valued telephone support services when asked, Janette built a fine business reputation.

However, due to a very heavy workload early on, Janette's accounting records were a little inconsistent. They were also presented to the tax authorities later than Janette had originally intended. As a result Janette was forced to spend two full days trying to account for the inconsistencies and was eventually charged interest on her tax debt due to it being paid late. Janette had learned her lesson the hard way and resolved to keep her accounts properly updated in future.

Lance loses the motivation to support his customers

Because of the problems Lance had selling his word processor, he soon lost interest in further upgrading the product. Several customers did contact Lance about the availability of further versions of his software, but he rarely answered their calls. Consequently, Lance and his word processor quickly lost favour and within three months sales had dried up altogether.

Furthermore, Lance's accounts had been prepared in much the same lack-lustre way. So much so that his accountant had to spend a lot longer than usual preparing his annual accounts and as a result presented Lance with an extraordinarily high bill for his accountancy services.

Having lost a lot of money, Lance finally decided to quit software development altogether, still wondering how someone with all his much-praised technical ability could have got it all so wrong.

DISCUSSION POINTS

1. How do you intend to build a solid reputation for yourself?

2. What business records do you intend to keep and how will you ensure they are kept up-to-date?

3. Your business accounts show you what costs you are incurring, what monies have been received and your overall profit. Apart from being extremely useful to you, the tax authorities may need to view them in order to assess your tax liability. How will you ensure that they are complete, accurate and tidy?

12
Making Money from
Computer Software

The remainder of this book demonstrates some of the many other methods of profiting from computer software. But first let us consider the feasibility of earning a full-time living from writing and selling software.

EARNING A LIVING

If you intend making a full-time living from writing and selling software, then at some point you will need to give up your current full-time occupation. This might be highly desirable, but stop and think a little. Is this really feasible?

One way of finding out is to consider your annual after-tax (net) income. If your software business is to wholly support your current standard of living, this is the net profit figure it must yield every year.

For example, Lance's current after-tax salary is £12,000 per year. His software, currently selling at £40 per copy, yields a profit (after costs and tax) of just £10 per copy. To reach an annual profit figure of £12,000 Lance will need to sell 1,200 copies of his software per year, every year. This means he must, on average,

- sell 100 copies of his software every month

- sell five copies of his software every working day (assuming there are around twenty working days every month).

For an individual or very small software company, this is quite a challenge. It might be possible but, given Lance's particular track record, it is extremely unlikely.

In view of this, Lance would do well to remain in full-time employment, and to write and sell his software in his spare time. If, by doing this, Lance was able to make, say, five sales per week, he would earn an extra and very welcome £50 per week – on top of his normal salary.

What you will need
It may well be feasible for you to eventually earn a full-time living from your software. Remember you will need

- a good idea

- sound project and marketing plans

- a quality product

- skilled advertising and selling techniques

- a quality approach to customer service

- accurate business and accounting records

- above all to keep the customer in mind at all times.

Now let us examine some other methods of making money from software.

USING YOUR SOFTWARE SKILLS

Your software skills can be used for far more than simply writing and selling your own software package.

There is currently a very strong demand from the UK business sector for individuals who can demonstrate an ability to design, write and test software, and companies are often willing to pay premium salaries to attract the kind of quality staff who can develop and run their computer systems.

Examining permanent IT job opportunities
The UK information technology (IT) sector currently employs over 300,000 staff. Over 280,000 of these are employed permanently by companies offering salaries typically between around £15,000 – £25,000 per year for computer programmers. For software analysts and designers the permanent IT market can be even more lucrative.

FREELANCING

Not all companies hire staff on a permanent basis. They also hire temporary freelance staff (freelancers) to work on various aspects of their projects. In the case study Janette originally hired two freelance programmers to develop her payroll software.

In fact, of the 300,000 staff employed in the UK IT sector around 20,000 are individuals working on a freelance basis, not permanently attached to any one company, but offering their software skills to a range of companies which make use of these skills as and when they require them.

When development work finishes, companies hiring freelance staff are able to quickly dispense with their services without having to pay redundancy money or find alternative positions for them. For the freelancers the task of continually having to find work and move from company to company is balanced by the relatively high rewards. On average a freelance programmer can earn around £1,000 per week on assignment. An average assignment lasts around nine months.

SPECIALISING

Whilst freelancers are hired to *carry out* the required tasks that companies have set them, the task of *advising* how work should be completed is normally the province of specialising consultants.

If your skills are specialised in some way, and you also have the ability to communicate them to others, then you could consider using your skills to provide companies with:

- advice (consultancy)

- training.

Offering your advice

Large computer systems and complex software packages are always a challenge to develop, maintain and use. Most companies will have a need at some time or other for specialist advice and guidance to help them overcome particular problems. When companies require such advice they often call in the services of consultants.

Consultants are specialists who have learned how to apply their technical skills to real business problems. They have also learned how to communicate their ideas and solutions to customers clearly and effectively.

Typically consultants initially study and then report on methods of approaching business or technical problems. Their advice often takes the form of a written report which is delivered to the customer at the end of the consultation. A consultant's report usually contains the following.

- A brief introduction or general overview of the problem.

- A full description of the main problem.

- A list of possible actions to take to avoid or deal with the problem, together with the consequences of such actions.

- A final conclusion and recommendation.

Consultants' advice does not come cheaply, particularly in the IT sector. On average a consultant can expect to earn around £300 – £500 per day during the length of the consultation period, typically lasting between one day and three months.

Typical consultancy tasks

Listed below are just a few of the IT-related tasks which consultants are often asked to give advice on.

- How to get maximum performance from existing hardware and software.

- How to deal with computer security issues.

- How to set up a computer system and its software.

- What hardware and software should be used for specific types of project.

- How to ensure that computer systems meet legal and auditing requirements.

- How to best solve particularly difficult hardware and software-related problems.

Training

People are not born with IT skills, they have to learn them. There is a healthy demand from business customers for IT-related training services.

A good trainer will both have a thorough knowledge of his own particular subject area, and an innate ability to impart this knowledge to an audience often having no prior knowledge of the subject.

Consequently freelance IT trainers can often earn between £200 and £500 per day for their services. For the companies themselves this fee is a small one compared with the costs involved with releasing an average of five to ten staff for between three to five days to attend the course. Without the necessary staff training there is also a significant risk that the project will overrun deadlines, or that a technically inferior product will be produced.

Did you know?

1. A single CD-ROM disk is capable of storing the contents of nearly 500 floppy disks.

2. Many computers with CD-ROM drives and sound cards are capable of playing ordinary music compact disks.

3. Most competent computer programmers are capable of writing a computer virus.

SUMMARY

Making money from selling your own software package or software skills is not only a real possibility, but also a perfectly feasible option for many different kinds of people.

The secret of success lies in careful preparation, thorough market research and a willingness to accept that all stages of your product's development should proceed according to the needs of the customer.

Start slowly, proceed carefully and realise that selling ability is as important as technical ability – probably more so.

With this in mind, now is the time to begin developing your own software package. Plan it, design it, write it, test it, then sell it. It could make you a lot of money and it will certainly be fun doing it.

CASE STUDIES

Dave continues to write games software

Dave eventually left his full-time job altogether, to concentrate on writing and selling his own software. His thorough technical knowledge and his willingness to learn how best to sell his software won him many admirers – and a living standard just a little higher than whilst working for his previous employers.

Dave never managed to write a top-selling game but this never bothered him. He had found his niche and was happy to live his life, creating and selling the computer games he had always enjoyed playing and using. As long as his hobby continued to provide him with a reasonable living, he would be content to continue doing what he had always done best – writing software.

Janette sells her payroll business and becomes a consultant

Janette's commitment to her customers eventually enabled her to build a business employing ten staff. She gained a solid reputation among her customers and was proud to say that none of them ever switched to another supplier during the five years she was trading.

Janette had always planned to continue writing and selling payroll software. That was until her business was noticed by a larger software company which offered her an attractive price for the whole of her business. After some negotiation, and assurances from the new company that her customers would not be adversely affected by the sale, Janette finally decided to sell her business.

She eventually moved into a consultancy role, offering her expertise and experience to companies developing financial software and operating computerised payroll systems.

Lance learns his lesson the hard way

Poor old Lance. Despite his technical ability he had never been able to make sufficiently high sales of his word processor to make a profit. At least he had never given up his full-time job to write software.

On reflection Lance came to realise that his main mistake was not talking to his customers. He also felt that his whole project had been undertaken on the basis that his technical skills would be enough to guarantee success. He now knew differently but had learned his lesson the hard way.

However, all is well that ends well. Six months later Lance had a new idea for a software package designed to help individuals and businesses navigate the Internet. After discussing this fully with several potential customers, he carefully designed and developed a quality, usable software product and, after attending a ten-week sales and marketing course at his local college, went on to make a respectable full-time living writing and selling his software.

DISCUSSION POINTS

1. Do you intend to earn a living writing and selling software? If so how will you decide when the time is right to go it alone?

2. Your software skills are valuable. Other than writing and selling your own software package how else might you use them to earn a living?

3. Writing and selling software is fun and can be extremely lucrative. However, building a profitable software business can also involve much hard work and it is possible that your efforts will bring you no financial reward. Does this deter you or are you going to try anyway?

Glossary

Add on An extra piece of software provided as an enhancement or improvement to an existing software package.

Analysis Study of business problems of customer requirements.

Application A computer program used for a particular purpose, or kind of work, like word processing.

Back up Additional copy of your software and data in case the information on your computer is lost or becomes unusable.

Beta test Final testing of a piece of software, usually conducted by users and customers rather than the software author just prior to final software release.

Bug Error in a computer program.

Bulletin board On-line information service, available to all computer users with a modem.

Bundling A marketing method used to sell two or more different software products altogether for a single price.

CD-ROM A round, silvery disk capable of storing huge quantities of information and which can be inserted into a computer.

Character set List of symbols used to represent a language, like English or Russian.

Computer Machine for running software.

Consultancy Giving specialist advice to others, usually on business problems.

Copy protection Mechanism for preventing the unauthorised use of a software product.

Copyright 'The right to copy'. A law which asserts an author's ownership to his or her work and which prevents others copying or otherwise profiting from it.

Cover disk Floppy disk or compact disk attached to, and sold with, a computer magazine.

Customer database Collection of information about customers.

Customers Buyers of products and services.

Customisations Modifications to software made for the benefit of individual customers.

Data Protection Act Act of Parliament passed in 1986 to protect individuals whose personal details are held on computers for business purposes.

Database Collection of information.

Design Plan for constructing a piece of software.

Device Piece of computer equipment.

Device driver A special piece of software, often written using assembly language, which controls the use of specific computer components (devices) like disks, screens and printers.

Documentation Paper- and screen-based instructions and reference material provided with software packages to help users use the software.

File A named collection of information held together and stored on magnetic disk, tape or compact disk.

Floppy disk Small, round, magnetic disk capable of being inserted into a computer and able to hold information.

Hard disk Magnetic device located inside a computer, used for storing information.

Hardware Term covering all forms of computer equipment like processors, hard disks, circuit boards, printers, monitors and keyboards.

Internet A popular on-line information service allowing access to the information held on computers all over the world.

Joystick Piece of equipment often used by computer games players to steer or control images on the screen.

Marketing plan Plan by which a business hopes to reach and attract its customers.

Mass market software Software which is likely to be of use to a large number of people.

Memory Temporary storage area inside a computer that is used to hold applications and data.

Menu List of available options or commands.

Modem Device enabling one computer to communicate with another.

Monitor Another word for a computer screen.

Mouse Hand operated device used to control a computer.

Press release Report to a newspaper, magazine or other publication notifying details of a newsworthy event.

Printer Device used for producing printed material.

Processor Device inside a computer used for executing computer programs.

Profit Amount of money remaining after monies spent have been deducted from monies received.

Program Series of computer instructions which together cause the computer to perform a specified task.

Program specification Document containing details from which individual computer programs can be directly written.

Programming The act of assembling computer instructions so that together they cause the computer to perform a specified task.

Project plan Schedule of events which specify the tasks and time scales involved with producing a software package.

RAM Acronym for Random Access Memory. Information and applications are stored temporarily in memory of this type. In any case they are lost if the computer is switched off.

Recommendation Suggestion made from one party to another, that a particular software package is suitable for use.

Referral Firm recommendation, almost an instruction, to use a particular piece of software.

Requirements Tasks people want a software package to handle.

Scanner Device for transferring images and text from paper and other media onto a computer.

Scrolling Movements (left, right, up, down) of the image displayed on screen.

Shareware Software provided on a 'try before you buy' basis.

Site licence Permission given by a software supplier to a customer to use an unlimited number of copies of the supplier's software package at the customer's place of business, usually for a single fee.

Software Collection of one or more computer programs.

Software development See 'Programming'.

Software features Capabilities and quirks of computer programs.

Sound card Device within the computer which allows it to generate sound.

Spreadsheet A special kind of computer program which allows the easy manipulation of numbers and text normally arranged in rows and columns.

Telephone support Facility provided by software suppliers which allows their software users to telephone for help or advice.

Testing Process of checking software to ensure it works as expected.

Time limited software Fully operational software which becomes totally unusable on a specified date or after a specified amount of time has elapsed.

Trade show Conference, exhibition or other gathering of people engaged in a similar line of business.

Upgrade Piece of software which has been modified, improved or enhanced since it was originally written.

Vertical market software Software which is only of use to a specific group of people like accountants or surveyors.

Virus An undesirable, sometimes disruptive computer program which attaches itself to other programs and often results in the computer becoming unusable or the loss of valuable data.

Word processor Computer program which can be used to write letters, reports or other documents.

Further Reading

COMPUTER MAGAZINES

Personal Computer World (VNU Business Publications). Monthly.
PC Plus (Future Publishing). Monthly.
What PC And Software (VNU Business Publications). Monthly.

COMPUTER TRADE NEWSPAPERS AND MAGAZINES

Computing (VNU Business Publications). A weekly IT newpspaer usually distributed free of charge to IT professionals on application to: The Circulation Manager, *Computing*, VNU Business Publications, VNU House, 32–4 Broadwick Street, London W1A 2HG. Tel: (0171) 316 9000. Fax: (0171) 316 9160.

Computer Weekly (Reed Business Publishing). A weekly IT newspaper usually distributed free of charge to IT professionals on application to: The Circulation Manager, *Computer Weekly*, Quadrant House, The Quadrant, Sutton, Surrey SM2 5AS. Tel: (01444) 441212. Fax: (01444) 445588.

THE SOFTWARE BUSINESS

How to Create, Publish and Sell Computer Software, Solomon Meyer (BBC Publications, 1986)
Writing Computer Software For Profit, A. J. Harding (Virgin Books, 1984)

MARKETING AND ADVERTISING

Success in Advertising and Promotion, John Milner (John Murray, 1995)
How to Produce Successful Advertising, David Farbey (Kogan Page, 1994)

Do it Yourself Advertising, Fred Hahn (Wiley, 1993)

How to Do Your Own Advertising, Michael Bennie (How To Books, 2nd edition 1996)

Marketing Plans, How to Prepare Them, How to Use Them, Malcolm McDonald (Butterworth-Heinemann, 1995)

The Marketing Casebase, Brian MacNamee and Ray McDonnell (Routledge, 1995)

How to Write a Press Release, Peter Bartram (How To Books, 2nd edition 1995)

SELLING AND CUSTOMERS

Who Dares Sells, Patrick Ellis (Thorsons, 1992)

How to Manage a Sales Team, John Humphries (How To Books, 1993)

How to Win Customers, Heinz Goldman (Pan Books, 1993)

Keeping Customers for Life, Richard Gerson (Kogan Page, 1993)

TECHNICAL

Introduction to Software Project Management and Quality Assurance, Darrel Ince (McGraw Hill, 1993)

Programming Languages, Paradigm and Practise, Doris Appleby (McGraw Hill, 1991)

How Computer Programming Works, Daniel Appleman (ZD Press, 1995).

RUNNING A SMALL BUSINESS

A Business Plan, Alan West (Pitman Publishing, 1995)

Lloyds Bank Small Business Guide 8th ed, Sarah Williams (Penguin, 1994)

How to Start a Business from Home, Graham Jones (How To Books, 3rd edition 1994)

How to Keep Business Accounts, Peter Taylor (How To Books, 3rd edition 1994)

The Best Small Business Accounts Book for a Non-VAT Registered Small Business, Peter Hingston (Hingston Associates, 1991)

How to Get the Most Out of Your Accountant, John Spencer (Mercury, 1992)

The VAT Guide (HM Customs and Excise, 1991)

Index

How to Manage Computers at Work
Graham Jones

Here is a practical step-by-step guide which puts the business needs of the user first. It discusses why a computer may be needed, how to choose the right one and instal it properly; how to process letters and documents, manage accounts, and handle customer and other records and mailing lists. It also explains how to use computers for business presentations, and desktop publishing. If you feel you should be using a computer at work, but are not sure how to start, then this is definitely the book for you... and you won't need an electronics degree to start! 'Bags of information in a lingo we can all understand. I strongly recommend this book'. *Progress/NEBS Management Association.*

160pp illus. 1 85703 078 8.

How to Start Word Processing
Ian Phillipson

In the modern world an ability to wordprocess is a valuable, even essential, skill. Even if you know little or nothing about modern technology, this book will help you, because it deals with basic principles. It is the ideal starting point for anyone who wants to know what is involved before committing themselves to a particular type of wordprocessor, or even enrolling on a wordprocessing course. If you want to design and print out simple letters and documents, produce mailshots, or explore desktop publishing, then this is the book for you, complete with case studies and checklists to help you on your way.

124pp illus. 1 85703 156 3.

How to Use the Internet
Graham Jones

The fast-growing Internet is set to revolutionise personal and business communications across the globe, as well as entertainment, information and education. Unlike other books on 'The Net', here is a down to earth practical guide that will really help you get the most out of this communications revolution. Using simple case examples, this book illustrates some of the many benefits the Internet can bring, and the personal, business or educational goals you can achieve. Soon, nearly everyone in the developed world will have access to the Internet. This book shows you how and where to begin.

128pp illus. 1 85703 197 0.